Put Thinking to the Test

Put Thinking to the Test

Lori L. Conrad
Missy Matthews
Cheryl Zimmerman
Patrick A. Allen

Stenhouse Publishers
Portland, Maine

I'm thinking I might have to use the text to get the other answer.

I will have to think like a scientist.

1

A student put the same amount of water into two bowls. He covered one bowl with plastic wrap and left the other bowl uncovered. He placed both bowls on the same windowsill. The bowls were left in the sun for several hours.

What **most likely** happened to the amount of water in the covered bowl? Explain your answer.

What **most likely** happened to the amount of water in the uncovered bowl? Explain your answer.

ow I'm thinking I might have to use B.K

My thinking is changing. And now I think I will have to compare them somehow.

I might have to get more information.

Synthesis helped me... think more thought-fully and I understood better. I did this because I could get my thinking down

Foreword by
Ellin Oliver Keene

Stenhouse Publishers
www.stenhouse.com

Library of Congress Cataloging-in-Publication Data
Put thinking to the test / Lori L. Conrad . . . [et al.].
   p. cm.
   ISBN 978-1-57110-731-2 (alk. paper)
   1. Educational tests and measurements. 2. Test-
taking skills—Study and teaching. 3. Thought and
thinking. I. Conrad, Lori L.

LB3051.P867 2008
371.26'2—dc22

                     2007049211

Cover, interior design, and typesetting by Martha Drury

Manufactured in the United States of America on acid-
free, recycled paper
14 13 12 11   9 8 7 6 5 4 3

As always, for Ed, Nathanael, and Emelia.
LC

For the loves of my life, Steve, Allison, Kyle,
and Rachel, who keep all of this work real.
MM

To my dad, my inspiration for speaking up.
CZ

To Trudle, Alice, and Judy—teachers all—
who taught me that children's eyes tell more
than any test ever will.
PA

CSAP

CSAP is easy
It truly is
you don't have
   to worry
Except if
   you're a
   teacher

by Christian
   Veeder

Not everything that can be counted counts, and not everything that counts can be counted.

ALBERT EINSTEIN

◆

Contents

Test Takers

Foreword

Is there such a thing as a truly original idea? Is it possible to generate new thinking? Has every inimitable concept already been discovered? We have so many superb professional books and articles in our field, it can seem as though all the great ideas have been taken! Remember raising your hand in class only to be preempted by the kid who got called on first? "She took my idea" was all you could say. The richness of available reading in education makes for tough going for would-be writers!

It's also true, and not necessarily contradictory, that when reading professional books and journals, I have a strong sense of déjà vu. I know I've heard or read this idea before and find myself reading along, longing to be surprised, shocked out of my assumptions, and forced to question my "knowledge" and beliefs. It is very difficult to capture that spirit in professional books. It's rare to read anything beyond a new variation on an old theme.

Rare, that is, until *Put Thinking to the Test*. I knew that Lori, Patrick, Cheryl, and Missy met frequently to discuss professional issues and that they were working on a book related to testing. I had no idea, however, that their proposal would be so fresh, so original, and, simultaneously, so sensible and immediately useful.

Essentially, Missy, Cheryl, Patrick, and Lori propose that teachers capitalize on what we know about comprehension strategy instruction in a high-stakes testing context. They suggest that as children learn to activate background knowledge, use mental images, determine importance, synthesize, monitor, infer, and question, they also learn to apply those thinking strategies to the tests they take. These authors take the notion of treating tests as a separate genre to a whole new level by arguing that, in teaching each comprehension strategy, we can teach children ways to apply the strategy in a testing context. They suggest that, rather than cramming endless hours of inane and often ineffective test preparation into the weeks (and, too often, months) preceding the test, children can gradually learn how to *think* like effective test takers—throughout the year.

In *Put Thinking to the Test*, the authors take us inside grade 3–8 classrooms to actually show how they have helped children become more test savvy as they learn to use the comprehension strategies. We are treated to detailed examples of children who actually become excited (yes, I said excited) about taking tests because they have learned to think about tests as intellectually interesting problems to be solved. This is not a book you'll close wondering how to actually do what the authors suggest. At the end of most chapters, a *possibilities* section suggests lessons and outcomes for integrating comprehension strategies into the testing genre. At the end of the book, you'll find a straightforward question-and-answer section that addresses some of the touchiest issues with great clarity. I can't imagine how the book could be more practical or immediately useful to classroom teachers.

Patrick, Cheryl, Lori, and Missy reveal their own struggles as teachers, parents, and staff developers trying to go beyond complaining about tests to crafting a set of solutions that never compromises student learning. They show how insights about their own learning processes are translated into the inquiry-driven lessons that help children face tests with confidence. You'll observe their transformation from educators who, like most of us, were perennially frustrated with the "testing culture" to efficacious and proactive teachers and staff developers with a very workable plan to keep tests from bullying children.

I know teachers will devour this book and will find its suggestions very usable. But I also urge principals, literacy coaches, curriculum directors, and other leaders to read *Put Thinking to the Test*. These authors actually propose an approach to test preparation that can preserve the best traditions of fine teaching. Leaders will find support for the argument that we needn't sacrifice effective instruction for higher test scores; teachers can continue to teach deeply and well *while* preparing kids for tests without compromising time for instruction or professional integrity. This is no small contribution to the field.

It may well be that it takes four authors—a mixed-doubles team, if you will—to drill down to a truly original idea, but they have done it! Cheryl, Lori, Missy, and Patrick have trod on virgin snow here, and every reader of *Put Thinking to the Test* will be the richer for it—as will their students.

Ellin Oliver Keene
October 30, 2007

Acknowledgments

Work that began over sandwiches and sodas has grown into the book you're about to read. It's been a grand adventure . . . one that's had many partners.

We thank our colleagues at the Public Education & Business Coalition. It was through our initial tentative exploration with Gari Meacham, Judy Hendricks, Angel Wolf, Karen Berg, and Kim Schmidt that the idea of this book emerged. Their feedback and encouragement was essential . . . and in never-ending supply. We also thank Rosann B. Ward and Suzanne Plaut, PEBC's president and vice president of education, for insisting we write this book. Their confidence in us and in the potential impact of this work made all the late nights and long weekends manageable. And to all the other staff developers and lab classroom teachers who make up the extended web of PEBC's professional development, we offer our sincere and deepest thanks. As this book unfolded, it was your wisdom that threaded through our words. We know that much of what we had to say was, and ever will be, directly and deeply connected to all we've learned with you and from you.

We thank Philippa Stratton for encouraging us to blend our four voices. And Erin Trainer for dealing with all the details.

We thank our teaching colleagues who opened their classrooms to this work. It was on your classroom canvases that many of these stories were painted. Especially Angel Wolf, Sarah Grubb, Lesli Cochran, Veronica Moreno, Rachel Rosenberg, Liz Swanson, and Andy Kaufman—without your generosity these pages just wouldn't have had a voice.

We thank our friends. They listened to our brainstorms, our questions, our concerns, our doubts. They read initial drafts and offered loving feedback. And when we started wondering whether we actually knew enough to write a whole book about thinking and testing, their unwavering confidence buoyed us. Without Troy, Susan, Ilana, Randi, Karen, and Kristin, our fellow Freaks, we might not have reached the end of this adventure.

We thank our families. The hours in front of computers, the missed soccer practices, and the cold dinners never shook their support. Our spouses . . . Ed, Steve, Kevin, Susan—thank you for your patience, your understanding and your love. And our children . . . Graham, Nathanael, Anneke, Sammie, Jensen, Carly, Emelia, Lauryn, Allison, Kyle, and Rachel— we hope our words make a difference.

We thank one another. We've remained good friends and even better colleagues. The laughter, the feedback, and the process have left us each better writers, better teachers, better people.

And finally, we thank our students. They are our inspiration, the reason we continue to strive to know more, do more, be more. They are always willing collaborators in our ongoing search for meaningful classroom practices. We believe in them. They deserve our best.

About Our Book

So, you think you want to write a book? Well . . .
What's it going to be about?
What ideas are you going to include?
How will it be organized?
How long will it be?
Who do you think will read it?
What are you going to call it?

Deciding to write this book . . . that was the easy part. Making all the other decisions that came along later proved to be the real work!

As a writing team, we wanted our efforts to reflect the kind of professional collaboration we prize. We know our best thinking happens when we're surrounded by colleagues. There's power in a group. So writing in third person made the most sense. Of course, we haven't done all the work we describe as a foursome—but all our talk over the past four years has created a collective memory from which we have drawn. However, when we retell a specific experience, lesson, or example, we strive to credit the individual team member who did the work.

We've organized our writing into three main sections.

Section One: "Wondering About Tests" outlines our early work with and initial insights about mandatory, high-stakes testing. In many ways, these three chapters represent a cementing of our strongly held beliefs about teaching and learning. In Chapter 1, "Coming to Know Standardized Tests: Walking in Our Students' Shoes," we share how through our own genuine inquiry we reacquainted ourselves with what it really means to take a standardized test. In Chapter 2, "Tests as a Genre: What Makes Standardized Tests Unique," we take our study into classrooms, helping students define the specific characteristics of tests, including the specialized demands of format, vocabulary, and testing procedures. In Chapter 3, "Increasing Student

Stamina: The Role of Workshop Structures in Becoming Successful Test Takers," we focus on the many ways classroom workshops help students develop the necessary metacognition and stamina for the kind of difficult, isolated work standardized tests often demand.

Section Two: "Thinking About Tests" describes the new territory we've explored, meshing thinking strategies and test taking. Each chapter in this section focuses on one thinking strategy. This way, readers can either read across the entire section or focus on the specific strategy that piques their curiosity.

Each chapter in Section Two includes three important features: Student Examples, Stories from the Classroom, and Possibilities: Craft Lessons for Teachers and Students. Including student work and retellings of actual classroom interactions is our way of honoring the brilliant work of our most important teachers: our students. The examples and stories come directly from classrooms across the Denver metro area. Listing additional lesson ideas is our way of extending these stories and samples. We frame these ideas as questions because taking an inquiry stance is essential for effective, authentic instruction. The lists aren't extensive because we know our readers will have smart ideas of their own that better match their students' exact needs. Our hope is that as you look through these work samples and read these vignettes and think about the lesson ideas, you see the possibilities of this work in your own classroom, with your own students.

Section Three: "Still Learning About Tests" brings closure to the story of our work. Chapter 11 offers our responses to questions we frequently hear and even ask ourselves about weaving thinking strategies with testing. And in the final chapter of this book, "Integrity: It's All About Being True to Ourselves and Our Profession," we come back to where our inquiry began. After all our reading, all our work in classrooms, all our talk, we realized that it boiled down to maintaining our integrity. The words of students, like sixth grader Jordan Allison, underscore the importance of sticking to what we believe.

In the face of testing pressures, our integrity is truly our final line in the sand.

04/07/2005   Douglas County News Press

Biggest Upside to CSAP*: No Homework
by Jordan Allison

Overview of CSAP
The CSAP window was open for me March 8–16. Our testing included math, reading and writing. I thought it was all pretty easy; except for just a few math problems that confused me and some reading Q&A that I figured out at the very last minute before my teacher said "STOP!"

The upside of CSAP: No homework and no regular confusing math work. We also got to have a pizza party as a celebration of finishing. The downside of CSAP: We have regular class work to make up. Thankfully, it'll be a while before I have to do it again.

I estimate that there will be about 353 more days before I have to take CSAP again.

Here's CSAP in four simple words: Boring, Uninteresting, Weird and Life threatening (ha-ha, just kidding!).

Now that I've finished taking CSAP I still wonder: Why do we do CSAP? How does it help us as students? We are actually learning things in school that are tougher than what is on CSAP, but does CSAP ever help us? Will CSAP actually get us somewhere?

Maybe, maybe not. One thing CSAP will teach us: How to take a test. We know how to fill in bubbles, and how to write a well-developed paragraph.

The day before we started CSAP our building resource teacher came in and gave us a pep talk about CSAP. She told us that CSAP is one-third skills, one-third strategies, and one-third psychological (how you think you will do on the test).

She told us that if you think you will not do well, you will probably end up not doing so well. On the contrary, if you believe that you will score way above advanced, then you might just get your wish.

I use this thinking not only on CSAP, but on other stuff too. On any kind of test I take, talent show auditions [I'm playing the piano], sports, swimming tests my endurance, this strategy helps me be positive.

*Colorado's yearly standardized test given to all students in grades three through ten.

Wondering About Tests

One place comprehended can make us
understand other places better.

EUDORA WELTY

◆

"Every river has its source . . ." So begins the acknowledgment page in the booklet *Thinking Strategies for Learners* published by the Public Education & Business Coalition (PEBC 2004). And, like all rivers there had to be a starting point for the work we've done with thinking strategies. What began as a trickle of initial work high in the Rocky Mountains has slowly grown into an intricate stream of thought, meandering to and among classrooms throughout the Front Range of Colorado and beyond.

The headwaters of our thinking began nearly twenty years ago with a body of research originally developed by P. David Pearson, Laura R. Roehler, Janice A. Dole, and Gerald G. Duffy. In their groundbreaking work we lovingly refer to as "Chapter Seven" (1992), Pearson, Roehler, Dole, and Duffy detailed a body of research describing what proficient readers do to make sense of text. Later referred to as the "proficient reader research," the authors fused the research about the *processes* proficient readers use when negotiating text and began to define the repertoire of strategies *all* readers employ when comprehending text. Their research became the boundary waters of instructional practices PEBC staff developers and lab classroom hosts have investigated, incorporated, and internalized, serving as the crux of our work with teachers and staff developers in eight major Denver-area school districts and many districts throughout Colorado and the nation.

The comprehension work was synthesized in Ellin Keene and Susan Zimmermann's book *Mosaic of Thought: Teaching Comprehension in a Reader's Workshop* (1997). Together, Ellin and Susan, along with several PEBC staff developers, took "Chapter Seven" and asked the big question, "So, what would this look like in the classroom?" The result?

- That comprehension can and should be taught explicitly.
- That we must understand how these strategies work in our own reading.
- That all readers can and should use these behaviors to better comprehend what they are reading.
- That by teaching the strategies we "give children the tools they need to exercise their critical thinking faculties, to struggle with human confusions, and to embark on their own explorations of the mystery and beauty of life." (Keene and Zimmermann 1997)

As a result of Ellin and Susan's brilliant work, we've spent time taking a closer look at the idea of comprehension as thinking. The results have meandered into unique tributaries permeating our own classrooms and the classrooms of teachers with whom we work. Since their original work, Keene and Zimmermann have written a second edition of *Mosaic* (2007) and several authors have broadened the strategies, extending them into the nonfiction realm (Harvey 1998), specific crafting lessons (Harvey and Goudvis 2000), the primary reader's workshop (Miller 2002), the 'tween years as writers (Morgan 2005), the arts (Mantione and Smead 2002), work in the library/media center (Grimes 2006), guidance for parents (Zimmermann and Hutchins 2003), math instruction (Hyde 2006), and even into specific content areas with high schoolers (Tovani 2000, 2004).

What has been discovered and replicated over and over is that to think critically and metacognitively, all learners, no matter the context, use the same behaviors. They

- ask questions;
- create mental images;
- draw inferences;
- synthesize new learning and ideas;
- activate, utilize, and build background knowledge (schema);
- determine most important ideas and themes;
- monitor for meaning and problem-solve when meaning breaks down.

Originally labeled as reading comprehension strategies, we've come to identify these behaviors as thinking strategies used by readers, writers, scientists, historians, mathematicians . . . and now test takers.

You know the scenario because it's become almost universal in classrooms across America: students opening test-preparation booklets, sharpened #2 pencils in their hands, teachers at the ready with scripted directions in proctoring mode; thoughtful teaching, student ownership, authentic experiences shelved until the "testing season" passes. In some classes, this "season" lasts a few weeks; for others it's an experience that occurs with increasing regularity across the entire school year.

And all in hopes that students will score higher on the test, that individual schools will fare better in the yearly berating by the local newspapers, that critics will be quieted, and that threats of wholesale school restructuring sometimes known as "reconstitution" will be avoided.

The four of us know these feelings all too well. Collectively, our teaching experiences stretch across nearly eighty years. We've worked with kindergartners, ninth graders, and every grade in between. We've taught in suburban classrooms and urban ones. Patrick and Cheryl have spent the majority of their time navigating the daily joys and quandaries of their own classrooms. Missy and Lori have stepped out of the classroom for a time to coach teachers and school leaders. Each of us has grappled firsthand with the trials of testing. And we've each struggled with contradictory, sometimes demeaning, results.

Because we're a group of educators committed to crafting learning experiences in which students are active participants in constructing meaning, committed to creating classrooms where activities are relevant and thinking-centered, and committed to maintaining the integrity of our own professional knowledge and ongoing reflection, we've refused to bow to the pressures of the "testing season."

We embrace the demands of shared accountability and student achievement. We applaud efforts to articulate essential learning and high expectations for all students. And we understand the role tests play in the world outside our classrooms.

But we refuse to put aside all we know to be good instruction, relinquishing precious instructional time and our own beliefs, so students can spend endless hours practicing tests.

Our purpose in writing this book is to recognize the fact that learners can and should use thinking strategies at all times:

- while reading independently during reader's workshop;
- while solving a math problem during mathematician's workshop;
- while conducting a scientific investigation;

- while composing a piece of writing;
- while researching historical events;
- and while taking a standardized test.

Strategic, active, flexible thinking occurs as learners make specific decisions to understand—especially when they negotiate the particular demands imposed by high-stakes, standardized tests.

Because we believe that all students are capable thinkers, and that teachers can provide rich, mindful learning experiences for their students, we've come to believe that we can't ignore teaching the kind of thinking that will help students succeed on standardized tests.

And because we believe this, we've written a book about testing. As you read, you'll come to understand that this book is not about

- creating "fake" activities that match a test;
- teaching to the test—or not teaching to it;
- raising test scores as a singular, all-consuming goal.

Instead, this book is about

- responding to the high-stakes testing environment in a professional, forward-thinking way;
- understanding the kind of thinking our students need to do well in any learning setting;
- honoring our own professional inquiry and integrity.

Chapter 1 Coming to Know Standardized Tests: Walking in Our Students' Shoes

At one time, the purpose of the public schools, at least theoretically, was to educate children; now it is to produce higher FCAT scores, by whatever means necessary. If school officials believed that ingesting lizard meat improved FCAT performance, the cafeterias would be serving gecko nuggets.

DAVE BARRY, *Miami Herald*, AUGUST 4, 2005

◆

Education, *Fear Factor* Style

By Cheryl Zimmerman

I admit it. I watched *Fear Factor*. I wasted an hour on Monday nights cringing at the sight of human beings eating rancid pig snout. The spectacle of a man shoving live sewer rats aside with his mouth in search of the key that will unlock the woman who lies trapped under buckets of belching bullfrogs—what better way to cure the Monday-night doldrums?

And, I admit it. I'm a teacher. No pig snouts or sewer rats in the classroom. No giveaway cars and no surprise trips to exotic islands. So why draw a comparison between *Fear Factor* and education these days? For me, it has something to do with stunts, time limits, elimination, and humiliation.

The months of February and March constitute high-stakes testing season in Colorado. Classrooms, like Hollywood sets, are modified for these "stunt" days. Wall displays disappear and open doors close. Productive hums turn to anxious hushes, and highly secretive testing materials appear from inside locked cabinets. Will it be harnesses dangling from helicopters this year, or maybe barred cages submerged in freezing pools? Enter the high-stakes testing contestants, our students. Like the opening shot of a *Fear Factor* episode, contestants approach the set, words reminiscent of *The Little Engine That Could* echoing in their ears. "I'm going to show 'em what I know. Like Mom said, I'll just do my best. I think I can, I think I can."

Fear Factor was a one-shot deal. If for 364 days a year a contestant showed no sign of arachnophobia, but signaled for help on stunt day as fifty hairy tarantulas crawled across his face, he was done. No do-overs or start-agains allowed. Strict standardized test rules don't allow for student do-overs either. If a student needs to leave to use the restroom, the test clock keeps ticking. And if an eight-year-old isn't at the top of her game on testing day because of a restless night, a bout with stomach flu, or a fight with a best friend, oh well. Her scores stand.

Neither *Fear Factor* contestants nor Colorado students have the luxury of time to complete their stunts. Too slow and you're taking the slow-motion walk of shame off the set. Too fast and you're likely to be penalized for stepping beyond the prescribed boundaries. Grab a post to steady yourself, that's a five-second penalty. Work beyond the stop sign on page twenty-two, that's a take-your-booklet-away penalty. Time flies when you're having fun.

Fear Factor contestants were eliminated immediately after failing a stunt. Reasons for elimination were obvious: half the cow-eyeball stew still remained in the glass when time expired. But because high-stakes test results aren't released for months, test questions fade from memory. Scores come back and students find that a mysterious number has all but eliminated them from the Honors Language Arts class or from Algebra II. Why? No one knows for sure. The actual evidence, the test booklet, is never to be seen again by students, teachers, or parents.

Remember the *Fear Factor* episode in which a blindfolded driver responded to oral directions from the passenger? The stunt involved maneuvering a car up a ramp and into the trailer of a moving semitruck. After what appeared to be a strong, straight-ahead start, the passenger repeatedly called, "LEFT!" as the blindfolded driver repeatedly cranked the steering wheel to the right. Minutes later the car rolled to a stop in the middle of a dirt field, yards from the target truck. Cameras caught every humiliating moment, up close and personal. How about the teachers and students working their tails off and still their scores aren't up to snuff? Scores are published and schools are ranked. Missed the target. Apparently, fear *is* a factor in the game of pulling funds and replacing unsatisfactory staffs.

I admit it. I was a *Fear Factor* fan and I am a public school teacher. Rancid pig snout makes me cringe. Training kids to perform a series of academic stunts in sixty-minute time slots makes me cringe. But 'tis the season, so let the testing begin. In the words of host Joe Rogan, "Are you ready? In five, four, three, two, one . . ."

◆ ◆ ◆

Like toddlers playing hide-and-go-seek, we initially responded to high-stakes accountability mandates by hiding under the blanket of what we knew to be instructional best practices. Surely no one would see us if we continued doing what we believed was best for kids. Surely no one would find us if we closed our classroom doors and kept on teaching. We attended the meetings, nodded in acknowledgment, and approached our work with the hope that the legislation mandating yearly testing would disappear.

However, after countless reminders from the media, in our schools, and in our neighborhoods, we eventually accepted the fact that the age of accountability and high-stakes standardized measures was a prescribed reality not likely to disappear anytime soon. The testing craze wasn't happening just in Colorado. It was a trend seen across the country. Each state was implementing some sort of yearly high-stakes achievement test. It became painfully obvious that hiding under the blanket wouldn't help our students know what to expect in these situations.

Many of our administrators and teaching colleagues responded to these new demands by proposing that we all implement testing activities. This created a new dilemma for us. These activities, no matter how positively intended, flew in the face of what we believed to be essential in our everyday work with students: authenticity and purpose. But at the same time, we didn't have a well-thought-out response to counter the idea of prepping for tests. We knew we weren't willing to take instructional time away from the types of learning experiences we valued most, but we weren't yet articulate enough to defend this position to others.

Leaning on a well-established professional ritual of gathering together to pursue questions that are both personally and professionally challenging, together with a small group of PEBC staff developers and lab teachers we decided it was time to figure out how to keep our professional integrity intact while helping students make sense of high-stakes tests. An inquiry study was born.

THE PATTERN OF LEARNING TOGETHER

Though the topics have changed over the years, our pattern for shared, collegial learning really hasn't. Whether working to better understand a workshop model, extending what we know about reading comprehension, or studying the ways literacy crosses content areas, our professional inquiry process has remained the same:

- We start with the things we find most mystifying in our daily work with students and teaching colleagues because these "rough spots" become the questions that anchor and fuel our studies.

- We find out what others have to say about our questions. Standing on the shoulders of learned colleagues has always helped us feel like we're part of a larger community of professionals trying to do the right thing for students.
- We engage in the actual work that sits at the center of our questions so we can understand it firsthand. After all, as Donald Graves taught us years ago, if the work isn't worthwhile for us, it can't be worthwhile for our students.
- We take our questions and initial thinking into classrooms so students can learn alongside us. Their insights inform, deepen, and shape our ongoing quest.
- We draw conclusions and frame answers to share with a bigger audience, always knowing that these answers are well informed, but tentative—we're never really finished because answers invariably lead to more questions!

OUR INQUIRY INTO TEST TAKING

How do successful test takers "do testing"? How does awareness of audience and specific requirements help test takers demonstrate what they know and are able to do? What does it take for test takers to maintain a strong sense of efficacy so they can walk into any testing situation feeling like Stuart Smalley: "I'm good enough, I'm smart enough, and doggone it, people like me!"?

With these questions in hand, we set out to learn what others were saying and writing about testing. Patrick Googled "standardized tests" and found dozens of websites and articles. Gari Meacham, a third/fourth-grade lab teacher, brought in a three-ring binder filled with test-prep materials her school district had distributed over the years. Kim Schmidt, another staff developer, gathered recent articles from *Language Arts* and *Phi Delta Kappan*. Angel Wolf, a lab teacher working in a tested grade level for the first time, brought in a worn copy of *A Teacher's Guide to Standardized Reading Tests: Knowledge Is Power* (Calkins, Montgomery, and Santman 1998). Cheryl brought a healthy dose of skepticism. Karen Berg, a media specialist and former classroom teacher, brought her whole-school perspective. Missy and Lori brought copies of a few released test items—samples initially used with students "released" to the public by various state departments of education—for the group to try. And Judy Hendricks, PEBC's beloved project manager, brought her very real belief that tests are a bad thing because they, in her words, "always made me feel stupid!"

Because we needed to see the structure of different tests, we gathered science tests and math tests, reading tests and writing tests. And because we

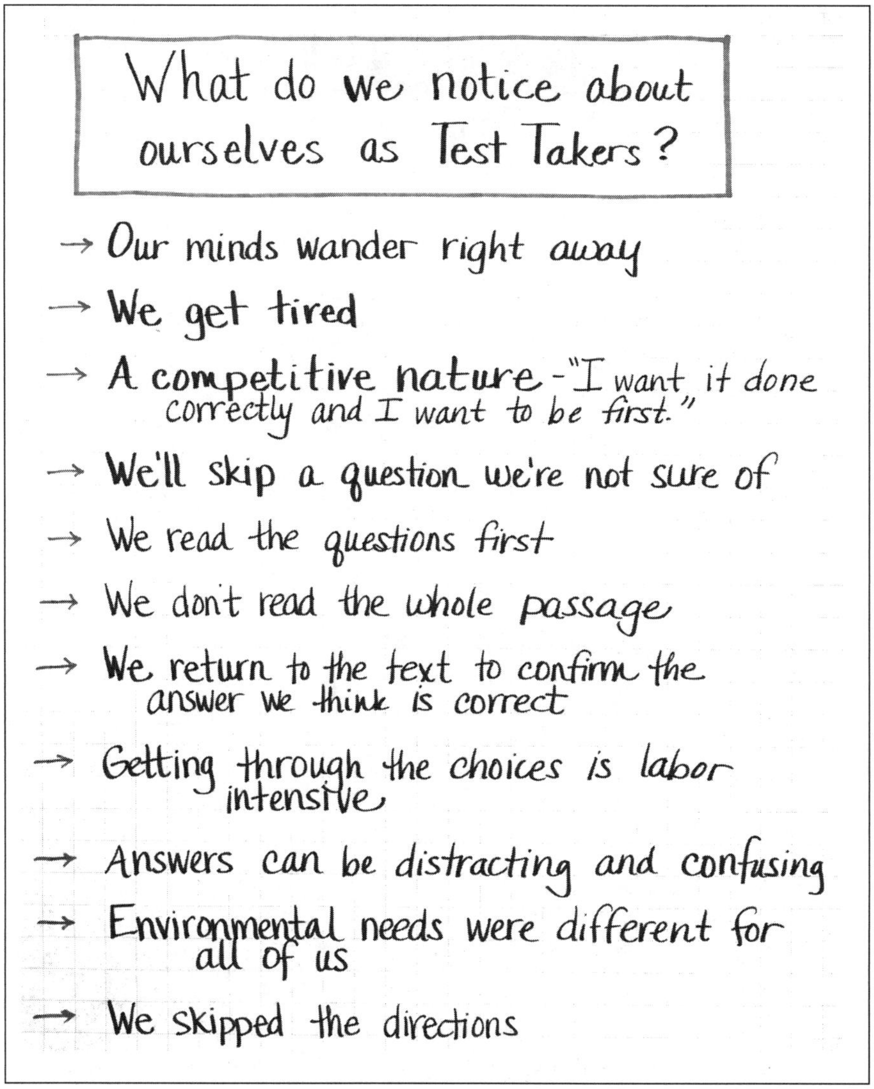

What do we notice about ourselves as Test Takers?

→ Our minds wander right away

→ We get tired

→ A competitive nature - "I want it done correctly and I want to be first."

→ We'll skip a question we're not sure of

→ We read the questions first

→ We don't read the whole passage

→ We return to the text to confirm the answer we think is correct

→ Getting through the choices is labor intensive

→ Answers can be distracting and confusing

→ Environmental needs were different for all of us

→ We skipped the directions

Figure 1.1. We charted our early reactions.

needed to do challenging work, we put aside test items originally written for elementary students and worked through items meant for middle and high schoolers instead. At one point, each group member read a different book or article about testing and shared common themes and interesting ideas. We also spent time talking with colleagues outside the group, collecting ideas from others who weren't spending so much time thinking about standardized tests. Their fresh insights gave us new perspectives and avenues to explore.

As we hunched over test items and read through articles, we recorded our thinking and charted our reflections. Our processes were far from automatic, and our findings were fascinating (see Figures 1.1 and 1.2).

Figure 1.2. Margin writing on a
practice test from one of our initial
inquiry attempts.

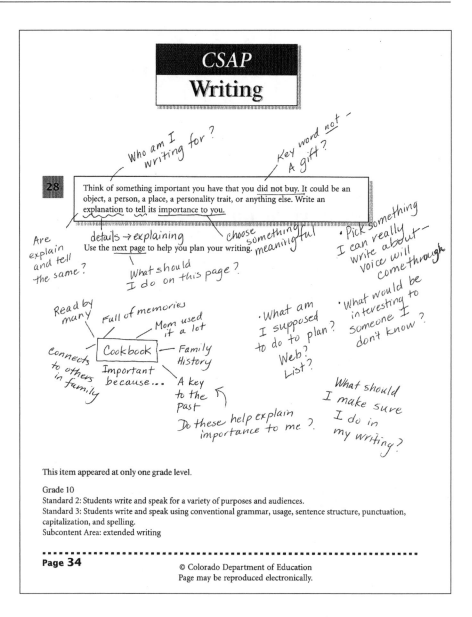

WHAT WE DISCOVERED . . .

After six months of reading, talking, and taking tests, we came to some
important conclusions—some confirming, some surprising, and some
worthy of further study. Our shared efforts validated our commitment to
thoughtful, strategic work with released items versus endless, mindless drill
on test-prep materials. It increased our drive to uncover our own truths
about test taking. And it deepened our empathy for what our students experience every spring.

Figure 1.2. *continued*

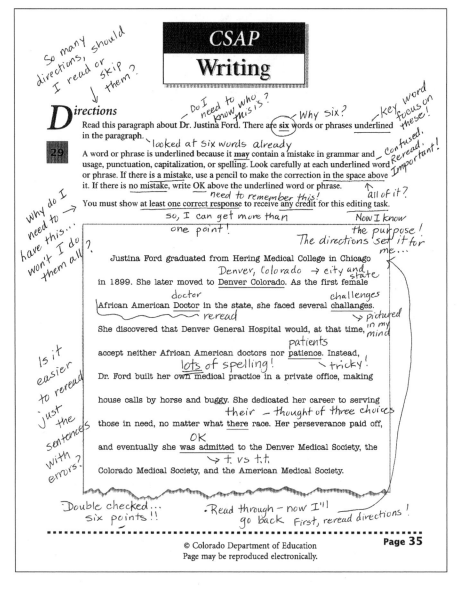

We suspected, and were pleased to discover, that being a good reader, writer, scientist, or mathematician went a long way toward being successful on a test. We effectively dealt with the high school samples even though we hadn't taken an English literature course or a biology class within recent memory. Confidence in our own reading, writing, and thinking made this unfamiliar work manageable.

We also happily noted that the range of text included in the various samples we tackled matched the range we provided for students in our classrooms daily, weekly, and monthly. We've always advocated for a rich, well-balanced reading and writing diet for our students. Believing that text variety increased students' interest, competency, and flexibility, we've worked to fill our classrooms with stories, feature articles, memoir, expository pieces, poetry, essays, scientific writing, and math problems.

These discoveries reaffirmed our bias that good teaching might indeed be 90 percent of the battle for getting good test scores. But we figured out more.

We were surprised by our lack of following the "golden rules" of test taking. We didn't all read the directions. We often found ourselves skipping around inside the various subtests. We also found ourselves having to regularly reengage in the test-taking process. Even though our interest in our inquiry study was very high, our stamina for this sort of isolating, on-your-own work was very low.

And we noted that tests really are a unique genre. They're not structured like a novel, even though they include fiction writing. They look different from a math textbook, even though they include number problems. They demand a particular sort of pacing to get to the end, which we typically don't use when reading a newspaper or magazine, even though they include similar article-type writing.

We found that all tests have

- genre-specific vocabulary;
- genre-specific format; and
- genre-specific procedures and requirements in terms of answers and timing.

And all of this is set within the content demands of the grade-specific test. (See Chapter 2: "Tests as a Genre: What Makes Standardized Tests Unique" for a further discussion on the genre-specific nature of standardized tests.)

We also realized that all the work we'd done in terms of comprehension and thinking strategies really did come into play. As we coded text and talked about our discoveries, thinking-strategy language filled the air and the margins of our tests. We found ourselves noticing the way a poet used pronouns to help us determine what was most important. We used specific test language to make inferences to help us answer questions about a short story. We activated our background knowledge about the relationship between fractions and decimals to complete a math section. We created a detailed visual image to support our making sense of a science subtest on soil erosion.

This sampling of our own processes led us to wonder: Are the thinking strategies we teach every day in our classrooms as tools for understanding everything from poems to math problems useful for accessing the world of standardized tests? Would these cognitive moves help students become active, strategic test takers? Would extending strategy instruction to include *thinking through tests* move us out of our role as passive, angry recipients of the testing craze?

These new questions became the catalyst for further study. Exactly how are the strategies we've come to understand so well as thinkers related to teaching students how to be savvy test takers? Our inquiry study took on a new look and a new sense of urgency, becoming the "hook" that made this sort of teaching palatable, even necessary, because it fell well within our definition of meaning-based, integrity-filled classroom practice.

We came to three very important initial conclusions:

- It is essential for us to approach test taking with our students the same way we did for our own learning—from the stance of shared inquiry.
- When we name our own thinking, what we need to teach students becomes exquisitely clear.
- We need to continue to build classrooms conducive to this kind of in-depth study—classrooms that exemplify a culture of thinking.

AND THE KIDS . . .

The old saying "out of the mouths of babes" takes on new meaning when listening to what students say about the ways standardized tests have become an overwhelming and often unwelcome part of their classroom experiences. We end this chapter with two letters written between Patrick and his oldest daughter, Anneke. As part of her weekly fifth-grade homework, Anneke was expected to write in her Nothing Book, a back-and-forth journal ostensibly designed to extend the famous question-and-answer exchange between parents and children everywhere: "What did you do in school today, dear son/daughter?" "Nothing, Mom/Dad."

The insight exchanged between Patrick and Anneke underscores the challenge thoughtful teachers, students, and even parents everywhere encounter thanks to tests' effect on schools.

Dear Mom and Dad,

How was your week? Mine was good. In math, we're still doing CSAP practice; it's giving me an aching headache! Also we're doing time tests every day. In reading today [Friday], we had a Read-a-Thon to celebrate Read Across America. In writing, we're also doing CSAP practice, it seems like everywhere I turn, I hear, or see the horrible, haunting word CSAP. Aaaaagh! I'm in Mrs. McKee's group for CSAP writing.

In history we're studying about colonies, and maps, and slavery. On C-track we got a mailbox so now I can write letters to my friends. I don't have to deliver them, so they stay a surprise. I've gotten four letters and written two.

Sincerely,
Anni

Dear Anneke,

CSAP, CSAP, CSAP . . . as Aunt Randi would say, "Oy vey!" I agree that it's haunting—isn't that just terrific! Wouldn't you rather be haunted by the sound of beautifully written text, the thrill of closing a novel with a tear rolling down your cheek, or learning about how Cynthia Rylant or Jonathan London or Eve Bunting use writer's tools in their work?

What's better than sitting in a group talking about A Taste of Blackberries, On My Honor, *or* Prairie Songs? *What's more important—learning to question text, to create sensory images, to infer— than learning about how readers comprehend? What's better than filling a notebook with dreams, and wonders, and memories? What's better than hearing a beautifully written poem, a laughing poem, and a poem that touches your soul? What's better than exploring your passions, your life topics, or just something you're interested in? What's better than "real" writing? I can't think of anything!*

Anni, I honestly despise what we're doing to learning in the name of CSAP. Is accountability important? Certainly! Should we measure growth? Certainly! But what are we doing to you—the learner?

Poor teachers—we're under such pressure, and we're throwing out research and the orthodoxies we hold dear with "the baby's bathwater"! And so, we see the joy of learning turned into hours of "stuff" just to "raise" scores. Sad. I guess I need to speak up as a parent—write to our fearless leaders and say, "Enough is enough!"

As a teacher, I feel nervous and jittery and nauseated at this time of year . . . and I know your teacher must be feeling the same way. As a parent, all I can say is "Do your best!" "Eat a good breakfast," and "Show what you know!" Mostly, I want to tell you I'm sorry!

In a few weeks it'll be over—until next year. Then you can get back to the real joys of learning, of being a child. It goes by so quickly, childhood. I want you to read, to write, to learn . . . and to enjoy being eleven. 'Cause someday you'll turn forty-two and feel the same tug in your heart that I am feeling writing this note to you . . . I just hope it's without the word CSAP haunting you!

I love you! If you score a partially proficient or advanced, you'll score what you're meant to score. Frankly, your score is not what matters to me. In the meantime, read a poem, sing a song, share a great story with a friend—let those be the things that haunt your childhood. We'll stand up and handle the rest!

Love,
Daddy

Chapter 2   Tests as a Genre: What Makes Standardized Tests Unique

*. . . if we think about the test as a sort of genre, bizarre though it is,
we could teach kids how to negotiate it in much the same way that we
teach them how to negotiate any other genre. Our goal was not to
have the kids practice the test over and over again, which we knew
tended to reinforce ineffective test-taking strategies. Instead, we
imagined a test sophistication study in which the students would
explore the unique qualities of this genre and learn how to respond to
its demands with speed and accuracy.*

DONNA SANTMAN

◆

By mid-September, the third graders in Cheryl's class were accustomed to
the workshop routine. After a rousing game of indoor hockey in P.E.,
they filed into the classroom and sat on the rug in the gathering area.

"So, you guys, we've noticed that taking a close look at a text together
helps us before we tackle the same sort of text on our own. We've looked at
poems, stories, and nonfiction articles. Today I'd like us to look at another
kind of text." Cheryl flipped the switch on the overhead projector. A sample
reading test item filled the screen.

"What's that?" Sam asked.

"Well, what do you think? What do you notice?"

Sam studied the screen. "There's a picture of a bird. It's hard to tell what
kind of bird it is. And is that a jar?"

"There's a title," said Shyla. "'Invite a Hummer to Lunch.' A hummer?
That's weird."

"There's something above the title. See where it says 'directions'?" Sonia
paused. "Why would there be directions?"

"Anybody willing to read the directions aloud?" Cheryl surveyed the
class. Many hands shot up. "Go ahead, Max."

"Okay, it says 'Directions. Read this article. Then answer numbers 1 to 9.' Why would someone have to tell us we should read the text? If we want to know what it's about, we have to read it."

"Max, it sounds like you're noticing that this is a different kind of text. We don't always see directions included in our reading. I'm curious to know what else you notice about this text." Cheryl placed a second page on the projector.

After a few seconds, Jack said, "That looks like how-to writing. It says 'to make a hummingbird feeder,' and then there are bulleted steps."

"Interesting, huh? It does look like the kind of writing you guys have been studying in writer's workshop. Now take a look at the third page."

"The directions said something about answering one to nine. I bet those are the questions."

"Good thinking, Sarah. What do you notice about the questions?"

"Some have choices. You can just fill in the bubble, I think. Some have a bunch of lines after the question." Sarah pointed to the two types of questions on the screen.

"So, you're noticing two types of questions. What do you think the purpose of the questions is?"

Alec raised his hand. "You know how we've talked about fake reading? You might look like you're reading but you're not really trying to understand? You couldn't answer the questions if you were fake reading. Maybe someone is trying to find out if you're really reading and understanding, so they're asking questions at the end."

"Thanks, Alec. As a matter of fact, this is a sample from a reading test. People write these tests—we'll call them test makers—and they are trying to find out if you're able to understand what you read. In class we show our understanding in lots of ways. We talk to each other, we jot our thinking on sticky notes, and sometimes we even draw or act to show our understanding. This kind of reading test requires readers to show their understanding by answering questions.

"I have a copy of this reading test sample for each of you. You may work on your own or in pairs. Spend about twenty minutes with the test. See what else you notice. You may jot notes and use highlighters to track your thinking. Be prepared to share when we gather back together."

Third graders scattered around the room. With clipboard in hand, Cheryl noted observations. The third graders studied the test for two days. Their work resulted in the chart shown in Figure 2.1.

Figure 2.1

What do we notice about tests?

- Tests include directions, many other kinds of reading don't.

- There are different kinds of questions. Some are multiple choice and some are constructed response.

- It's smart to look back at the text when you're trying to answer the questions.

- Rushing leads to absent-minded work. Metacognitive test takers take the time to pay close attention.

- The test evaluators won't come to our school to meet us in person so that we can explain our thinking. We have to show them our best thinking on the test.

1. In this article, "nectar" is another word for

O   the painted red flower

O   syrup

O   honey mixture   *Multiple Choice max*

O   a feeder

2. Which of these would be the **best** newspaper headline for this article?

O   Honey Mixture Causes Diseases in Birds

O   Red Flowers Have Lots of Nectar

O   Wash Your Bird Feeders!   *multiple choice max*

O   How to Make a Feeder for Hummingbirds

3. Explain why you should paint a red flower on your feeder.

max Constructed Response

_____

_____

_____

_____

_____

4. Why do you suppose the author suggests you build a feeder if you want to watch hummingbirds?

O   because building feeders can be lots of fun

O   because many hummingbirds are starving

O   because a feeder will attract the hummingbirds

O   because it is fun to trick hummingbirds with red painted flowers

↑ Ridiculus answer max

5. What is the **most likely** reason the directions call for a special kind of red paint?

O   This kind of paint won't be ruined in a rainstorm.

O   This kind of paint is the cheapest.

O   Birds like the smell of this kind of paint.

O   This kind of paint is the same color as most hummingbirds.

6. According to the article, if you were all out of sugar would it be OK to use honey instead of sugar?

O   Yes

O   No

Now explain why:

_____

_____

_____

_____

Figure 2.2

The thinking her students jotted around various test items underscored these collective insights (see Max's thinking, Figure 2.2).

As this story from Cheryl's class shows, tests aren't like the other sorts of print we ask students to access every day. Tests may include poems, science experiments, and math problems. Tests might invite students to write about their thinking or respond to a story's theme. And tests will probably challenge students to explore content in which they aren't yet proficient. But because standardized tests are structured for the sole purpose of quantifying what students know and are able to do, they sit in a category all their own. Helping students understand a test's unique characteristics increases the likelihood that they will approach a testing situation with confidence and a clear sense of purpose.

As part of our initial inquiry into standardized tests, we read pieces detailing what makes tests different from other reading material. Janet Allen

7. In the chart below, number the steps in the correct order given in the article on how to build a bird feeder. The first step has been done for you.

ORDER	STEPS
	Wrap some wire around the neck of the jar.
	Wash your feeder every four days.
	Paint a large red flower around the hole in the lid.
1	Hammer a nail through the lid of a jar to make a hole.

Go back and Re-Read

8. According to the article, what do you need to build your feeder? *max*

O   wrench

O   pliers

O   tape

O   sandpaper

9. Read this instruction.

Make "nectar" for the feeder by stirring 1/2 cup of white sugar into 1 cup of boiling water.

Which picture shows this instruction?

O   O   O

(2002) talks about students being "test-smart language users." Jim Cummins (2000) explores ways we can help students develop the academic language involved in standardized tests. Lucy Calkins, Kate Montgomery, and Donna Santman (1998) address the importance of teachers and their students being test savvy. And Amy Greene and Glennon Melton (2007) provide lesson ideas that encourage teachers and their students to explore tests with the mindful eye they would use with any other sort of print.

The thinking of these expert colleagues anchored our initial work with students, helping us reconfirm that tests are indeed a genre of their own with

- a unique format and particular way of treating content;
- a specific set of vocabulary students don't typically find in their daily classroom work;
- particular procedures students have to follow.

FORMAT AND CONTENT

Tests aren't like any other kind of stuff we read. They don't look the same and we can't do them the same. They're kind of weird, but I like them!

DREW, FOURTH GRADER

◆

Tests aren't put together like other texts. They don't have the heft of the novels that fill our classroom libraries. They aren't as colorful as the picture books we often use for our craft lessons or the range of the poetry we share across the year. They don't include the same sort of supporting information our math books do, and they certainly don't have the allure of the websites our students regularly scour when researching. But they're a part of our classrooms. It's our job to help students become familiar with the many ways tests differ.

Over the years, each of us has used *book frenzies* to introduce a new genre to our students. Sitting in a big circle, with new texts stacked in the middle, our students choose a book, spend a few minutes perusing it, and then pass it to the person sitting next to them. After five or six passes, the books are returned to the middle of the circle and we generate an initial attribute list. We've used this process to define literary nonfiction, biographies, memoirs, how-to books, and single-author collections. The point of "doing a frenzy" isn't in-depth study but to get a quick, general sense of the genre's setup and format, whetting students' collective appetites for further, more careful study.

Since we agreed with Calkins, Montgomery, and Santman (1998), that many of our students' "difficulties [with the test] would dissolve if they were to learn more about the format of the test" (97), we decided to do this same process (frenzy followed by generating an attribution list) using a collection of sample tests and released items. This sort of engaged, open-ended search lighted our students' curiosity. It took time, but we knew simply handing our students a list of test attributes would be ineffective, contradicting every other genre study we'd ever crafted.

So, as part of a larger inquiry into the ways standardized tests look, feel, and sound, we invited our students to take a first cut at the samples we laid out for them, developing a general sense of how the tests were put together, how they used page space, and how we might go about "reading" them. In this way, released test items became mentors for our study.

What our students initially noticed was very predictable:

1. The sections we have to read are usually short and are followed by questions.
2. Many of the questions are multiple choice with circles to bubble in.
3. Some of the sections start on one page and continue on another.
4. Some of the reading sections are printed in columns like a newspaper.
5. Some of the questions sit directly below very short parts.
6. A lot of the possible answers for math are similar.
7. The places to write answers are outlined or there are specific lines to use.
8. Directions are listed in a few different places, but usually at the beginning of each test section.
9. There are direction words like *go on* and *stop* at the bottom of most pages.

As we studied the tests more carefully, additional content and format attributes emerged, some of which proved contradictory to long-established classroom patterns.

We value authenticity in our classrooms. We make every effort to engage students in the real kinds of work readers, writers, mathematicians, historians, and scientists do in the world outside of school. We expect students to collaborate, use resources, demonstrate understanding in a variety of ways, and take the time necessary to produce high-quality work. Sadly, our students quickly realized that standardized tests did not reflect these same expectations. Test work was very different.

While working through excerpts from various reading tests, our students found some important differences between what they did every day in our classrooms and how they were expected to perform on test days. They knew that readers didn't typically jump from one text to another in a prescribed amount of time, and that readers rarely demonstrate their understanding by answering multiple-choice questions. High-stakes tests require readers to do just that. There's no opportunity to discuss the text with fellow readers. And although helpful when working to understand, jotting notes in the margins of the text, underlining sections to remember or rethink, and highlighting portions to revisit are not allowed.

And reading subtests weren't the only places where our students discovered glaring differences.

Many high-stakes writing tests require test takers to edit random passages and to select the correct topic sentence for partial paragraphs. Real writers rarely, if ever, engage in such activities. Of course, knowledge of grammar, punctuation, capitalization, and spelling is an important part of a writer's repertoire, but that knowledge is demonstrated where it truly counts—within a piece of writing. High-stakes writing tests often require test takers to respond to prompts within a specified time limit and within a given number of lines. The use of resources such as dictionaries, thesauruses, or fellow writers is prohibited, yet in the world outside of school, writers rely on such resources all the time.

Beyond classroom walls, people use math as a tool to accomplish a task or solve a problem. High-stakes math tests consist of a string of unrelated items. A great deal of reading and writing is required, and problems are often awkwardly worded. A student who is a competent mathematician but an emerging reader or writer may not demonstrate math proficiency—not because she doesn't know the math, but because she can't read the text surrounding the actual math task. In our classrooms, we ask students to record their math thinking because this evidence informs our instructional next steps. Test evaluators are not responsible for making teaching decisions, so little space is provided on the test for recording thinking, and sometimes only the answers are required.

Real scientists engage in the work of answering big questions and creating new scientific knowledge. The recent discovery of the golden-mantled tree kangaroo in Indonesia demonstrates our ever-changing body of knowledge. Scientists don't rely on memorized facts and figures. They're out in the field observing or in the lab conducting experiments. In contrast, high-stakes science tests are relegated to paper-and-pencil tasks. Students must rely on an unrealistic amount of memorized content to answer test questions. And, like math tests, a great deal of reading and writing is required, lessening the chances that a struggling reader or writer will truly demonstrate his science competency.

After spending many days studying tests, our students' list about "What Makes a Test a Test" grew to include such things as the following:

1. There's a specific amount of time for each part of the test—and this time limit forces a test taker to maintain a certain pace because finishing is a have-to.

2. There's no way to really justify an answer, so overthinking actually hurts a test taker's score.

3. Being right is more important than being thoughtful.

4. Being able to read and write is as important on math and science tests as it is on reading and writing tests.

5. Many of the usual ways we can check and clarify our thinking are "off limits" during a test.

6. Knowing the purpose and remembering the requirements of the audience is huge.

7. The directions often hold important "keys" to showing what we know in the way the test evaluator will accept.

8. Being flexible in terms of "bouncing around" from one task to another is important.

9. The kinds of decisions test takers make are different and have to be made more quickly than decisions we make in regular schoolwork—the decisions are about how to approach each test section or task.

Recognizing and naming the many content and format differences between typical classroom reading, writing, math, and science and the items on high-stakes tests paved the way for grand conversations with our students, and, on our part, some explicit instruction. But in addition to content and format, we discovered that in a very real way, tests even use different kinds of words.

Student Examples—Noticing Format and Content Issues

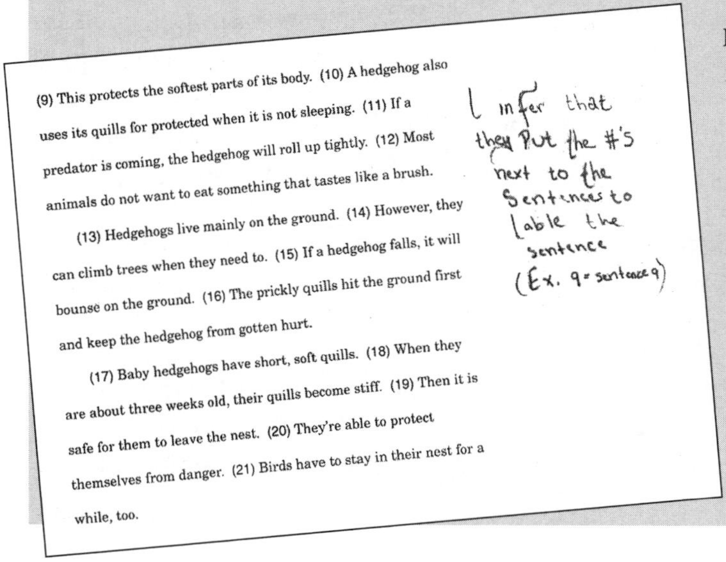

Figure 2.3. Jessica sees that, unlike typical nonfiction text, these sentences are numbered.

(9) This protects the softest parts of its body. (10) A hedgehog also uses its quills for protected when it is not sleeping. (11) If a predator is coming, the hedgehog will roll up tightly. (12) Most animals do not want to eat something that tastes like a brush.

(13) Hedgehogs live mainly on the ground. (14) However, they can climb trees when they need to. (15) If a hedgehog falls, it will bounce on the ground. (16) The prickly quills hit the ground first and keep the hedgehog from gotten hurt.

(17) Baby hedgehogs have short, soft quills. (18) When they are about three weeks old, their quills become stiff. (19) Then it is safe for them to leave the nest. (20) They're able to protect themselves from danger. (21) Birds have to stay in their nest for a while, too.

Handwritten note: I infer that they put the #'s next to the sentences to lable the sentence (Ex. 9 = sentence 9)

Student Examples—Noticing Format and Content Issues

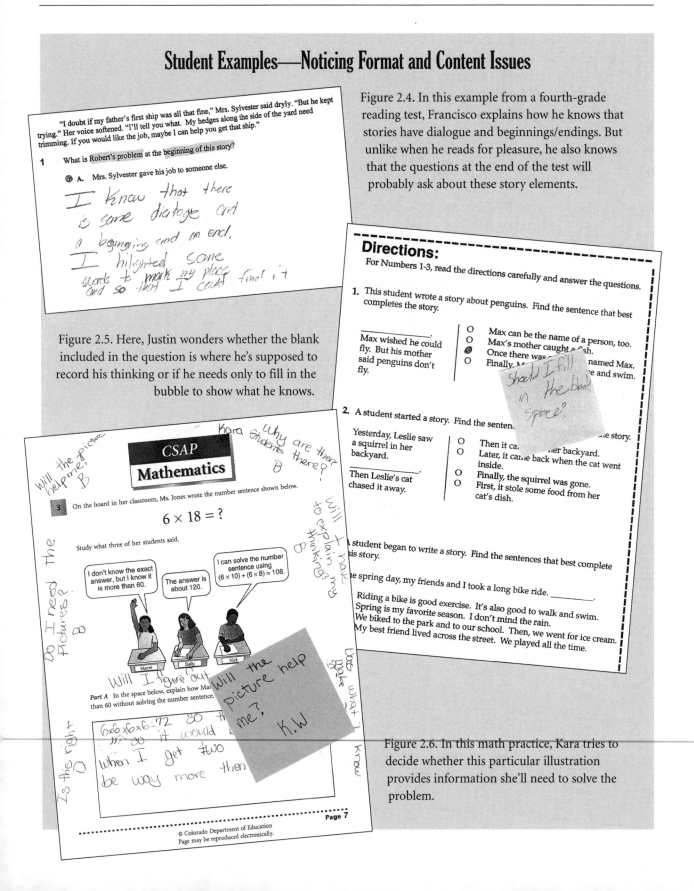

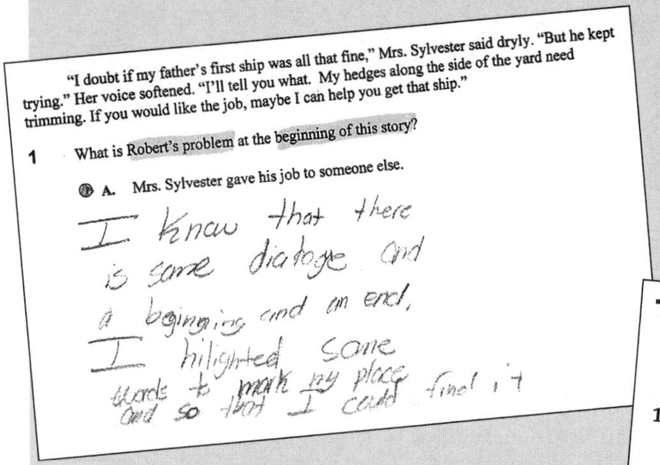
"I doubt if my father's first ship was all that fine," Mrs. Sylvester said dryly. "But he kept trying." Her voice softened. "I'll tell you what. My hedges along the side of the yard need trimming. If you would like the job, maybe I can help you get that ship."

1 What is Robert's problem at the beginning of this story?

A. Mrs. Sylvester gave his job to someone else.

I know that there is some dialoge and a begining and an end, I hilighted some words to mark my place and so that I could find it

Figure 2.4. In this example from a fourth-grade reading test, Francisco explains how he knows that stories have dialogue and beginnings/endings. But unlike when he reads for pleasure, he also knows that the questions at the end of the test will probably ask about these story elements.

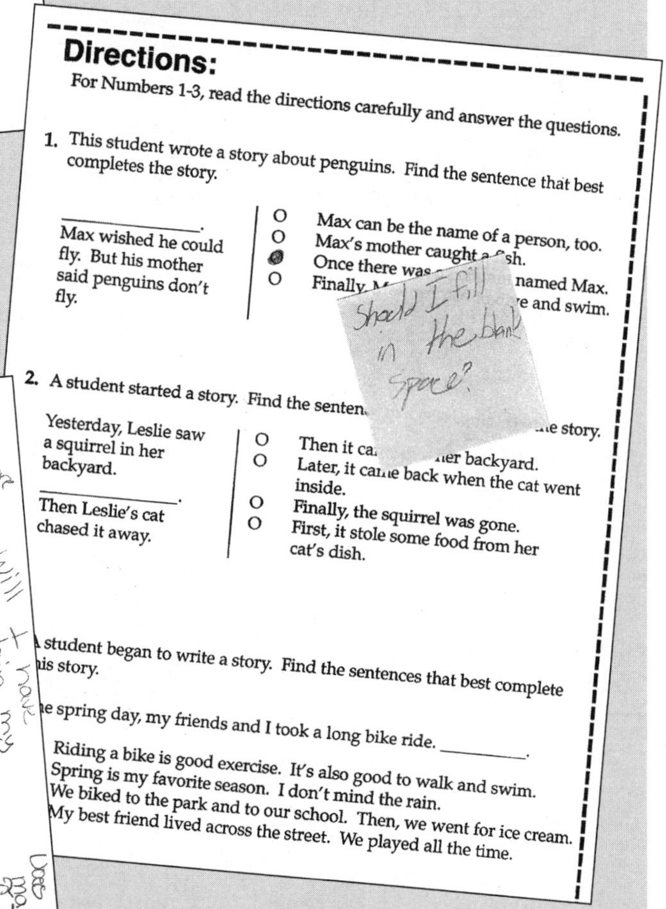
Directions:

For Numbers 1-3, read the directions carefully and answer the questions.

1. This student wrote a story about penguins. Find the sentence that best completes the story.

Max wished he could fly. But his mother said penguins don't fly.

- Max can be the name of a person, too.
- Max's mother caught a fish.
- Once there was … named Max.
- Finally, … and swim.

Should I fill in the blank space?

2. A student started a story. Find the senten… the story.

Yesterday, Leslie saw a squirrel in her backyard. ______. Then Leslie's cat chased it away.

- Then it ca… her backyard.
- Later, it came back when the cat went inside.
- Finally, the squirrel was gone.
- First, it stole some food from her cat's dish.

A student began to write a story. Find the sentences that best complete this story.

…e spring day, my friends and I took a long bike ride. ______.

- Riding a bike is good exercise. It's also good to walk and swim.
- Spring is my favorite season. I don't mind the rain.
- We biked to the park and to our school. Then, we went for ice cream.
- My best friend lived across the street. We played all the time.

Figure 2.5. Here, Justin wonders whether the blank included in the question is where he's supposed to record his thinking or if he needs only to fill in the bubble to show what he knows.

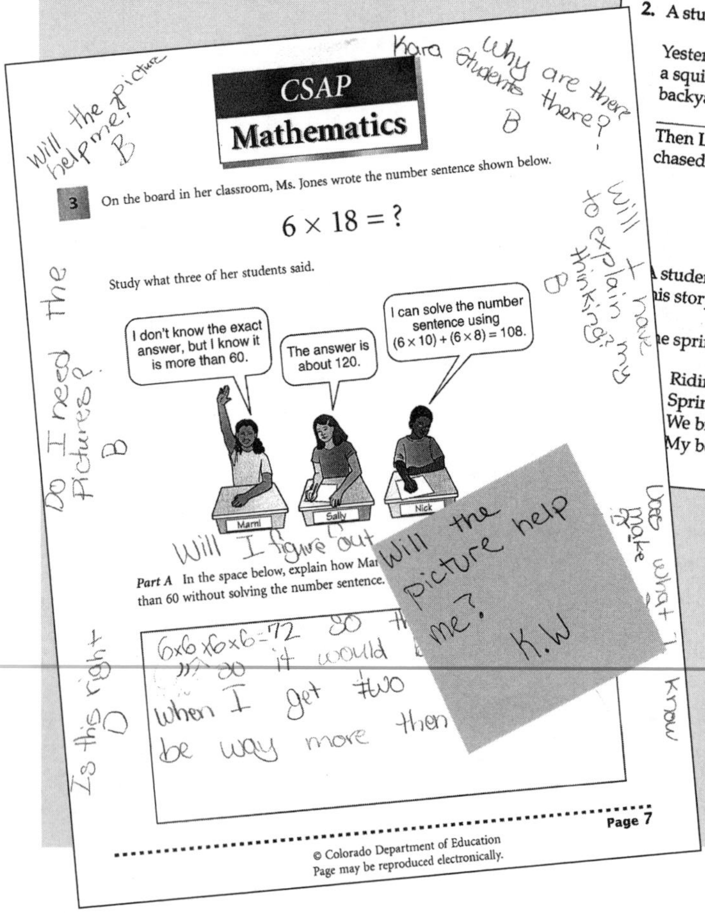
CSAP

Mathematics

3 On the board in her classroom, Ms. Jones wrote the number sentence shown below.

$$6 \times 18 = ?$$

Study what three of her students said.

I don't know the exact answer, but I know it is more than 60.
The answer is about 120.
I can solve the number sentence using (6 × 10) + (6 × 8) = 108.
Marni
Sally
Nick
Kara
Why are there students there? B
Will the picture help me? B
Do I need the Pictures? B
Will I have to explain my thinking? B
Will I figure out
Will the picture help me? K.W
Is this right
Does make what I know

Part A In the space below, explain how Mar… than 60 without solving the number sentence.

6x6x6x6=72 so … it would … when I get #two … be way more then

Page 7

© Colorado Department of Education
Page may be reproduced electronically.

Figure 2.6. In this math practice, Kara tries to decide whether this particular illustration provides information she'll need to solve the problem.

TEST-SPECIFIC VOCABULARY

*I talked with the kids a little about how they'd probably find funny
words on the test that they'd never see anywhere else. You know, words
like* passage *and* most likely *and* in order to. *But then when we were
in the middle of the test, one of the questions used the word* besides.
*The question asked for important things about soccer from the
reading* besides *what was listed at the beginning of the article. Almost
every one of my kids answered the question with examples from the
whole text, so they were doing exactly what we'd been working on . . .
using information and ideas from the actual test to answer the
questions. But because they ignored that* besides *most of the answers
are going to be counted wrong. Next year, I really need to do more
than just mention that tests have a language all their own!*

JAMIE, THIRD-GRADE TEACHER

Many researchers have highlighted the importance of helping students
become very aware of test-specific vocabulary (Allen 2002; Calkins,
Montgomery, and Santman 1998; Greene and Melton 2007). Janet Allen goes
so far as to say, "high-stakes testing is a harsh reality for them [students] and
the harshness is increased when the vocabulary of the questions impedes
understanding" (56). These experts make it clear: relying on the rich word
work and vocabulary development we do every day isn't enough when we
want our students to be successful on standardized tests. We need to do
more. We need to have students be on the lookout for *test words*—language
that Calkins, Montgomery, and Santman (1998) call "super- or hyper-
English."

With highlighters in hand, we asked our students to restudy the test
samples we'd been using. This time, however, instead of naming formatting
and content issues, we asked them to hunt for words they didn't know or
hadn't seen before in their day-to-day work as readers, writers, mathematicians, and researchers. Eager to do this sort of hide-and-seek work, students
dug back in to revisit the tests they'd come to know.

Later, we read through what our students had highlighted, looking for
patterns we could use for future teaching. Here are a few of the vocabulary
topics we found:

Noticing New and Difficult Words in Test Questions

After exploring multiple test samples, we discovered that many of the most
challenging vocabulary words didn't show up in the test sections themselves.

The really tough words, such as *suggests, passage*, and *expresses*, were written into the questions—with the potential to overload any test taker. To extend this initial discovery, we began collecting these difficult words, creating companion lists of "everyday synonyms" to match. This helped broaden our students' vocabulary in general, support their emerging test wisdom, and build a sense of "word wonderment" that rolled over into other areas of their daily learning.

Being Ready for Questions That Ask What Specific Words Mean

On almost every reading test our students explored, at least one question was dedicated to defining a word from the passage. The questions often went something like, "What is the meaning of *guffaw* in paragraph 21 of the story?" As they came to expect questions like this, our students soon realized they could use the same unknown-word strategies they use when encountering new words in any reading setting; they had to be ready to look at word parts, parts of speech, and the passage context. But they also realized they'd have one additional strategy they couldn't use in "real reading": trying out the possible answers listed after the question to determine which word made the most sense. This work became an intriguing game—except when the answer options were also unknown words! When this occurred, students quickly realized that once again, getting the right answer seemed more important than understanding the reading.

Becoming Word Collectors

Over and over again, current research describes the benefits of building a broad, diverse vocabulary. When students notice new words, sorting them into various categories and moving them from *new* to *owned*, they develop a learning disposition toward language. They become word collectors. Applying this to our work with tests helped students develop a sense of control even in a potentially out-of-their-control testing situation.

As our students began sorting test vocabulary, they noted the same sort of categories Janet Allen (2002) suggests in her work with middle school language arts students: "literature terms, writing vocabulary, reading words, grammar and usage terms, vocabulary terms and testing prompt words" (56). However, we found that combining *grammar and usage* and *vocabulary* made sense. And, because we were working with test examples that included math and science items, we added two categories specific to the content of those subjects: *math terms* and *science words*. We also added a final category, *thinking cue words*, because we noticed that test makers used certain types of words to "cue" the test taker.

Figure 2.7

Test Vocabulary ... Our Sorted List

Literary Terms
fiction / nonfiction
opinion
theme
narrator
story
beginning / middle /end
essay
characters

Writing Vocab
writing process
compose
initial / final draft
well-developed
revision
audience
cross-outs
tell /explain
paragraph /multi-paragraph

Thinking Cues
predict
most important
best describes/ best explains
most likely
according to
purpose
based on

Reading Words
problem
support
details
opinion
captions
author's purpose
main event

Math Terms
manipulatives
total
angle
how many
rule / pattern
label
difference
table / chart
mean /median/mode
difference

Grammar/ Usage Terms
subject / predicate
phrase(s)
capitalization
sentence
punctuation
interjection
spelling

Test Prompts
session
writing task
text box
scoring criteria
selection (s)
booklet
extended response
passage
short answer / multiple choice

Science Words
effect
controlled
investigation
system
diagram
hypothesis
procedure

As our lists grew (see Figure 2.7), it became clear to our students that developing their vocabulary made taking a test easier. They knew what words to expect, when to use their general word-level strategies (such as "make a meaningful guess," "read to the end and come back," and "use letter sounds and word parts"), and when to employ their specialized "testing vocabulary."

Because there will always be new tests with new ways of saying the same thing and asking the same question, there isn't a "magic list" of words to drill into our students. Instead, when we study tests as a genre of text, it's important for students to understand that "successful test takers must be able to translate the unique language of the test" (Greene and Melton 2007).

Student Examples—Noticing Test Vocabulary

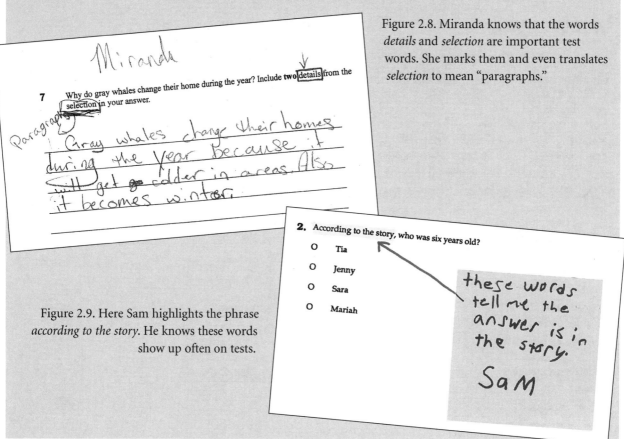

Figure 2.8. Miranda knows that the words *details* and *selection* are important test words. She marks them and even translates *selection* to mean "paragraphs."

Figure 2.9. Here Sam highlights the phrase *according to the story.* He knows these words show up often on tests.

TEST-SPECIFIC PROCEDURES

I love this kind of work. It's like detective work.
KELLEN, FOURTH GRADER
◆

As a child, Lori watched her father use the same "planful" procedure for reading the daily newspaper. A career insurance salesman and self-proclaimed sports expert, Chuck found a specific process for making sense of the newsprint that landed on his doorstep each morning:

* First, he'd skim the first two pages of the front section. That way, he'd have enough information to carry on a conversation about the day's news abroad.

- Next, he'd turn to the obituaries. Chuck would carefully scan the last names on the off chance that one of his policyholders had died and he'd need to begin the long process of filing claims and processing death benefits.
- Finally, Chuck would settle in to read every detail of the sports section. He wanted to absorb every fact and figure so he could speak with great authority about who should win the next football game or what chance the local high school basketball team had of repeating as state champion.

The procedure was always the same—when it came to reading the newspaper. However, Chuck's process for understanding other types of text, the newest life insurance actuarial tables, for example, varied wildly. He knew that different texts demanded different "game plans"; reading everything the same way at the same pace just didn't make sense. Taking tests should be just as *planful*—and successful test takers know that tackling a test demands a specific plan.

Through our study, we discovered a handful of procedures students needed so they could effectively manage any test they might encounter. These included the following:

- how and when to use directions (e.g., when a test taker can ignore them, like when the directions are followed by a collection of straightforward computation problems, and when a test taker absolutely must read them carefully, like when the directions appear to be multistep or out of the ordinary)
- ways to eliminate possible wrong answers ("red herrings") when taking multiple-choice subsections (e.g., noting that in many computation problems one of the answer options is the correct answer using a different operation, narrowing the possibilities to two out of the four offered)
- developing an "internal clock" so pacing each timed section feels manageable
- using a few of the test questions to set an initial purpose(s)
- learning how to move back and forth between test sections/tasks and test questions without losing your place
- looking back into the test to verify answers or to find specific "test language" to use in extended responses

As our list of test procedures grew, so did our students' belief that they could negotiate even the most challenging testing situation. Just like Lori's dad, Chuck, they had a well-developed "game plan" for tackling any test put on their desks. They knew the rules and how to go about getting to the end. They knew tests were a distinctive genre complete with a unique format and way of presenting content, specialized vocabulary, and particular procedures test takers use to get from the first set of directions to the very last bubble.

Student Examples—Noticing Procedural Issues

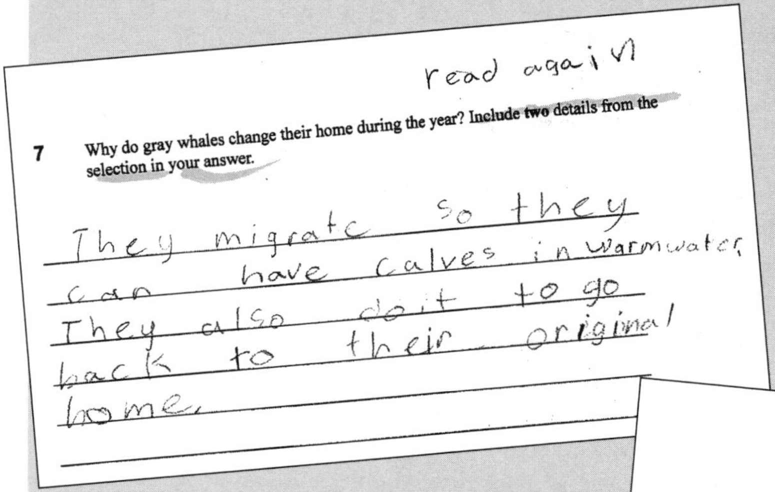

Figure 2.10. As a savvy fifth-grade test taker, Phoebe knows that when answering test questions, rereading is an essential strategy for finding the right choice.

read again

7   Why do gray whales change their home during the year? Include two details from the selection in your answer.

They migrate so they can have calves in warm water. They also do it to go back to their original home.

Figure 2.11. Isaac, a third grader, notices the page layout on a math practice test.

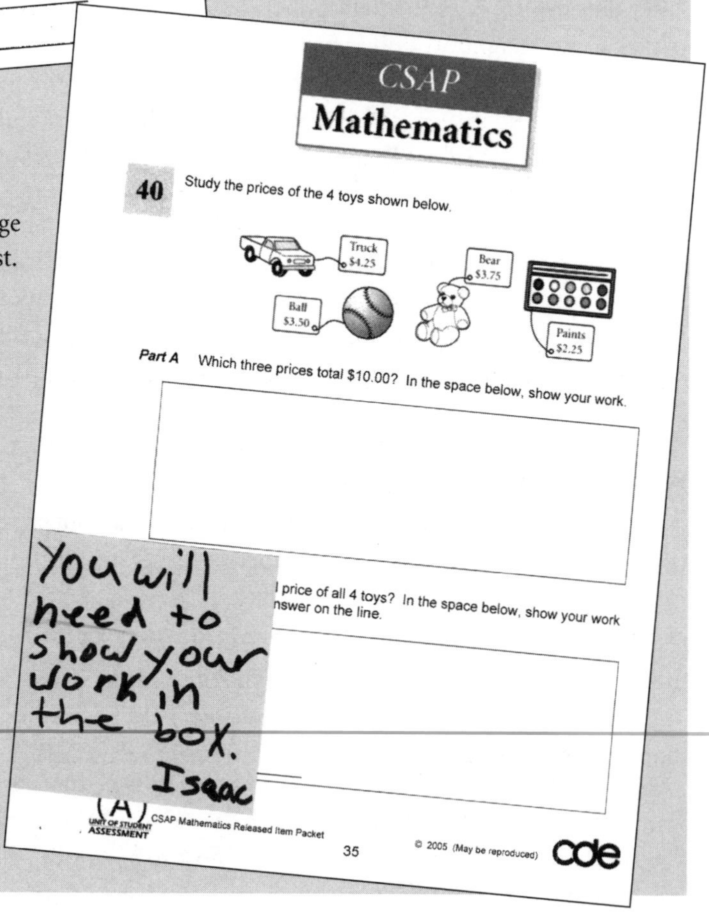

CSAP
Mathematics

40   Study the prices of the 4 toys shown below.

Truck $4.25
Bear $3.75
Ball $3.50
Paints $2.25

Part A   Which three prices total $10.00? In the space below, show your work.

price of all 4 toys? In the space below, show your work nswer on the line.

You will need to show your work in the box. Isaac

(A)
UNIT OF STUDENT ASSESSMENT   CSAP Mathematics Released Item Packet
35   © 2005 (May be reproduced)   cde

EXTENDING THE GENRE STUDY: TESTS AS PART OF OUR LIVES OUTSIDE OF SCHOOL

As with any genre study, we hope our study of tests will create a long-term impact. This means it's essential that we help our students explore the ways tests live outside the confines of school. For students to see test study as more than just a game to please, or even just appease, the school adults in their lives, we needed for them to see the power of knowing how to navigate tests beyond the classroom.

Not long ago, Cheryl's oldest daughter, Sammie, decided to pursue her scuba-diving certification. Cheryl's youngest daughter, Carly, decided to try out for the company group at her dance studio, and Cheryl's husband, Kevin, undertook a lifelong dream of learning to fly an airplane. All three pursued these goals outside of school or work. All three encountered tests along the way.

In Cheryl's third-grade classroom, her students name the many ways tests are a part of their lives outside of school. Michael, an avid snake enthusiast, remembered his dad giving him a test to see if he could hold a snake safely. Luckily, he passed the test and was allowed to continue searching for snakes in his neighborhood. Michael's classmate Samantha took a test at a pet store to see if she'd be a responsible adoptive parent for a guinea pig. Sarah took a test at the ice rink to advance to the next skill level, and James expects a test at the beginning of the swim team season each summer.

Tests happen at lacrosse practice, on the basketball court, and in the music studio. Picture the line of sixteen-year-olds at the Department of Motor Vehicles, each anxiously awaiting her driver's license test. Tests happen. Why not teach students how to approach tests—whether in school or outside of school—in a thoughtful, strategic manner? Sharing these stories takes some of the shock out of the high-stakes tests students encounter in school.

WHAT DOES ALL THIS MEAN NOW?

When we began our journey to understand standardized tests, we really thought of it as a solid genre study to be tackled a few weeks before our state test. But as our understanding grew, these initial notions began to change. In their text, *Guidelines for Teaching Middle and High School Students to Read and Write Well* (2000), Langer and her colleagues list a number of activities that support integration of test preparation into instruction:

- Analyze the demands of tests.
- Make overt connections between and among instructional strategies, tests, and current learning.

- Develop and implement model lessons that integrate test preparation into the curriculum.

It still makes sense to investigate tests as a unique genre with students who are in their first testing year. For those of us living and teaching in Colorado, that means third grade. But for school years beyond third grade, where students bring with them schema about standardized tests, this sort of genre-specific instruction needs to be more integrated across the year and should focus not only on the attributes that make tests different from other classroom work, but more important, on how proficient thinkers go after tests in a strategic way. Released items have a place in our classroom all year long, not just in the weeks leading up to the testing window. They are mentor texts, like well-written poems, math problems, and scientific explanations, to be analyzed and commented on. This approach puts standardized tests in a more balanced, less "everything else about authentic teaching and learning stops until the testing season has passed" position in our classrooms. And it helps students recognize the similarities and differences between test reading and every other sort of reading they come across in their daily lives in and out of school.

STORIES FROM THE CLASSROOM

Exploring Poetry from a Testing Stance

by Lori L. Conrad

Angel Wolf's fourth-grade classroom was filled with evidence of all the learning that had occurred over the past two weeks. Baskets of poetry collections lined the gathering spot in the front of the classroom. Individual books of poems sat on most every student's desk. The walls were covered with student discoveries and insights:

- a chart comparing poems to "cousin" texts—picture books about the same content but written in a narrative style
- a chart listing the students' emerging definition of what poetry is and isn't
- a chart naming the tools poets routinely use when composing poems
- anchor poems complete with student commentary

Writers' notebooks overflowed with original poems that matched specific craft lessons and a "Poet's Tip Sheet" Angel had adapted from Shelley Harwayne's 2001 text, *Writing Through Childhood*.

As I gathered the children together, I knew they had a clear vision for poetry, both as readers and writers. I also knew that helping them name the ways in which standardized tests make use of poems would both add to and contradict the experiences they'd been having for the past couple of weeks.

"It's clear from all the evidence in the room that you all have been doing some pretty deep thinking about poetry, how to read it, how to write it, how to learn from it," I said. "Today, my questions are these." I wrote these three big questions in the middle of a clean piece of chart paper and then drew a Venn diagram directly below.

1. Compared with our daily reading and writing work, how are poems treated differently when we find them on tests?
2. How are they treated the same?
3. And, most important, how does our thinking have to change when we encounter poems in a test packet instead of in a bound collection?

I labeled one circle of the Venn "Poetry in the World" and the other "Poetry on Tests."

"I've got some released items here where the questions are all based on poems. Your job is to read the test passages, and as you do, to take note of what's the same about your reading and thinking and what's different. You can record your thinking on these sticky notes. Pink sticky notes for all the ways reading poems on tests is like reading poems during reader's workshop. Green sticky notes for the things you notice that are different."

The kids grabbed sticky notes and stacks of released items and headed off to their tables.

After Angel and I gave the kids a few minutes to dig in, we began conferring with individuals.

"Adison, what are you noticing?"

"Well, on the tests, the lines in the poems are numbered. I've never seen that in any of the books we've read. I'm guessing it's because the questions ask about a specific line. Having the number there tells me where to look. It's easier than reading real poems because I don't have to read through the whole poem to answer some of the questions. I don't have to think about the whole thing like I do when I'm reading poems here in class. I just have to look at that one line. To get the right answer, you don't have to understand the whole poem."

Looking up from his work, Jacob added, "I can pay more attention to a poem when it's not on a test because I'm not thinking about what I need to do with the answers. I can pay more attention to what the poet wanted me to think, and make pictures in my mind."

"Say more about that, Jake," I asked.

"Well, poets want me to think 'what can I understand about this?' The test makers want to see what I know by answering their questions. My job changes. They're [the test makers] trying to see if I understand the questions they wrote—not really if I understand the poem."

Molly quickly added, "When I'm reading poems myself, there's a real freedom. I get to decide what to think about. On a test it's like we're all supposed to speak with one voice. It's about getting it wrong or right. What they say is right."

Patrick was a bit more pragmatic in his thoughts. "In our classroom, we read poetry collections. On tests, there aren't enough poems to be a collection. And it seems like tests don't use all the different fonts and spacing to grab our attention the way real poems do. Maybe it's because test makers don't really care about grabbing us. They know we have to read the poems on the test."

"Yeah, but these poems are kind of like cousins, like some of the poems and picture books we've been reading," Kellen added. "I bet the questions are going to ask how they're alike or something. That's what we did at the beginning of our study of poetry."

After the fourth graders finished their exploration, we all gathered back on the floor to fill in the Venn diagram.

"Maybe we need another color sticky—one for things that are the same with both test poems and real poems," Maureen suggested.

After handing out some blue sticky notes and giving the students time to record a few ideas, we began to gather ideas (see Figure 2.12).

Angel and I were once again amazed at the depth of their noticings. But it also left us with some questions:

1. How can we help students do this same sort of "comparison" with the other types of text that show up on tests, such as fiction, nonfiction, math story problems, and science experiments?
2. How might we extend this work to include prompted versus self-generated writing, including what to do when students are prompted to do silly writing they'd never choose to do in the world?
3. How can we continue to provide rich, extensive experiences with a wide array of texts so students walk into any testing situation with a sense of "I've seen that before and I know how to manage it" balanced with a healthy sense of "but I know it's going to be different because this is a test"?

How are poems treated differently on tests?

How does our thinking have to change?

How are they treated the same?

POETRY IN THE WORLD

- can take up more space because we aren't worried about fitting it on a page – Tanner

- when you read real poems you can express yourself and get it wrong and never care because real is free – Molly

- don't have questions after them – Anthony

- when I read real poems I know I get it because I laugh or cry... that's what the poet wants me to do – Dominique

- you choose what to read – Carsyn

- you have to think more because you have to think about the whole poem and there aren't questions to help you figure out what you're supposed to think about – Adison

- you don't have to prove you understand it to anyone but yourself – Kamren

- they can be about the same things... like seasons – Emelie

- they can have pictures – Tanner

- they can both use everything I know about how poems are set up – Kellen

POETRY ON TESTS

- you have to think what the test makers think – Adison

- somebody else chooses these – Dominique

- the test makers are always asking you questions – Drew

- in a test poem I am thinking more about what will come out of this poem later – I am also thinking what the test makers want me to think – Jacob

- you wouldn't generally have these questions in poetry that's real unless you asked them yourself – Molly

- you have to pay attention differently – Carsyn

- they can have things like onomatopoeia – Kamren

- they can have things like rhyming and line breaks – Anthony

Figure 2.12

Chapter 3 Increasing Student Stamina: The Role of Workshop Structures in Becoming Successful Test Takers

. . . the term workshop *harkens back to the ancient crafts-place,*
where not only did products get made, but education went on as the
master craftsman coached apprentices.
STEVE ZEMELMAN, HARVEY DANIELS, AND ART HYDE

◆

Testing situations are different from typical classroom situations. They have to be. They have to produce results that are reliable and valid for many students across many schooling contexts. And yet, it's the difference between regular classroom experiences and testing experiences that causes such a rub for many of us.

Imagine the message to students. "You've done *school* like this for the past seven months, but for this week, you can't. You'll have to do *school* differently. In fact, taking these tests won't be anything like the work you typically do." What a confusing message.

Testing situations require high stamina for demanding, unfamiliar work. Testing sessions can last anywhere from forty-five minutes to more than an hour. During these long blocks of time, students are asked to read materials and work on activities they haven't chosen, for which they may have very little background knowledge, and that may be beyond their instructional reading level.

Also problematic, students are required to work in isolation. In what other settings would we ask children and adolescents (the most social beings of all!) to work without talking to peers or gaining insight from adults? Students are required to be self-regulating and self-motivating for amounts of time well beyond what's considered typical in most classrooms.

The time we spend with our students has to help them anticipate and envision the work they'll do in testing situations. "Stamina matters a great deal on a reading test. It's a problem if the day a student takes a reading test is the first time he has been expected to continue reading for over an hour" (Calkins, Montgomery, and Santman 1998, 62). Classroom workshops help build those bridges from daily, in-depth, thoughtful work to the isolating demands of standardized tests.

A LITTLE BACKGROUND: HOW WE DEFINE A WORKSHOP

Call it a labor of love. The four of us have spent our careers studying and defining for ourselves what it means to teach using a workshop model. Donald Graves, Ralph Fletcher, Linda Rief, Jane Hansen, and Katie Wood Ray have mentored us as we've explored this powerful instructional framework.

For us, the workshop model defines how time is spent in a classroom. It's a predictable structure useful for any content learning. Thanks to Ellin Keene's initial thinking (see Keene and Zimmermann 2007 for a complete description), we've come to understand that there are three distinct components essential to any workshop: a craft lesson, composing time, and reflecting (see Figure 3.1).

Figure 3.1 A Workshop Structure

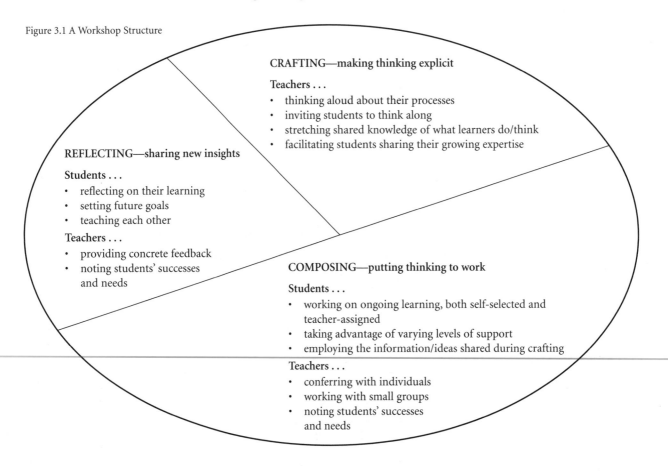

CRAFTING—making thinking explicit

Teachers . . .
- thinking aloud about their processes
- inviting students to think along
- stretching shared knowledge of what learners do/think
- facilitating students sharing their growing expertise

REFLECTING—sharing new insights

Students . . .
- reflecting on their learning
- setting future goals
- teaching each other

Teachers . . .
- providing concrete feedback
- noting students' successes and needs

COMPOSING—putting thinking to work

Students . . .
- working on ongoing learning, both self-selected and teacher-assigned
- taking advantage of varying levels of support
- employing the information/ideas shared during crafting

Teachers . . .
- conferring with individuals
- working with small groups
- noting students' successes and needs

CRAFTING

A workshop almost always begins with a craft lesson. This is the time when the entire class gathers for intentional, explicit instruction. Teachers use this time to introduce new concepts, content, strategies, or procedures. Craft lessons may include

- teacher or student think-alouds;
- work with a shared text or problem;
- fishbowl demonstrations;
- public conferring between a teacher and a student.

The goal of a craft lesson is to build collective knowledge of strategies or skills being studied over a period of time.

COMPOSING

As the craft lesson ends, composing begins. During this time, the longest portion of the workshop, students work individually or in small groups applying the craft lesson's content to their ongoing learning. The classroom teacher spends most of this time in one-on-one conferences, collecting data, and providing individualized instruction. The teacher may also guide the learning of small groups gathered together based on an identified common need or interest. Conferences and small-group work provide insight for the teacher about the progress of individuals as well as the entire class. This information can then be used to make instructional decisions.

REFLECTING

The workshop ends with reflecting. As students wrap up their individual and small-group work, they gather together as a whole class or in small groups to consider their new learning, refined thinking, and emerging understandings. Whole-class shares make it possible for everyone to learn from the insights of a few. Whip-around shares, quick "round the circle" responses from each student, invite everyone's voice into the room. Pair shares or small-group shares make more intimate interactions possible.

INCREASING STUDENT STAMINA: STUDYING STANDARDIZED TESTS IN A WORKSHOP SETTING

The power of a workshop comes from the predictability that teachers and learners expect, according to Katie Wood Ray in her book *Wondrous Words* (1999).

The beauty of the writing workshop lies in its predictability. Students come to know very quickly how the workshop works and what its components are. They know that there will be some time when they will meet as a whole group, a larger block of time when they can work on their own writing, either alone or with a group of peers. They know that during this time their teacher will be moving about conferring with various ones of them. They know that near the end of the block of time known as writing workshop, they will probably meet back together as a whole group, either to share from the day's work or to get one more bit of writing advice from their teacher. . . . Writing workshops need to be predictable places so that wonderful, unpredictable things can happen in them. (211–212)

We believe this predictability and routine have important implications for test takers as well. A workshop extends students' study of tests as a genre. It offers time to engage in challenging, important work long enough to gain meaning. This "stick-with-it-ness" helps build the kind of stamina learners need to be successful test takers.

CRAFT LESSONS—THINKING ALOUD

Test preparation, in the traditional practice booklet sense, has been surprisingly void of one important aspect: instruction. We've asked learners to read the passages and choose the correct response and come together in the end to check answers. We've reminded students to go back and review their answers if they finish the test early. We've gone over the publisher's official "testing hints" listed at the beginning of each practice test. We've shared key words such as *justify, clarify,* and *explain.* But we haven't *taught* the thinking behind the test.

Like any other content in our curriculum, testing demands explicit instruction. Students need instruction about the characteristics of this genre: the forms, vocabulary, and procedures as discussed in Chapter 2. However, beyond these logistics, students need to see and hear proficient test takers in action.

Think-alouds are an opportunity for learners to gain insight into what otherwise might be a mystery—how a test taker makes sense of testing material as he's taking a test. Putting language to our cognitive moves, the often automatic mental decisions we make, lets students see what is usually hidden. As you'll read in the vignettes in Section Two, we often think aloud, using a sample test item with our students gathered in close proximity. Having a very clear purpose for what needs to be modeled, we narrate what's happening in our heads so students can actually "see" our thinking. We intend to have our thinking become a scaffold for how our students may tackle similar work. The language of a think-aloud might sound something like this:

"Last night I was looking around on the Internet and I found this reading test sample. I want you to listen to the conversation I have in my own head about how I decide what's most important on a test. This will lead us to explore the differences between what's important in the reading we do each day and the testing items we see every now and then.

"As a test taker, I'm always trying to figure out what the evaluator is going to want to know about me. One of the ways I get a sense of this is by the kinds of questions that are asked. So, I'm thinking the questions are actually the most important part because they'll help me determine what's essential in the passage. In this question, 'What is paragraph four mainly about?,' the most important part is 'mainly about.' It's really a main-idea kind of question, and I know I'll have to make an inference about the main idea and rule out unreasonable choices.

"And this question, 'Look at the outline below and answer the question that follows,' has me looking at a partially completed outline. They've left the first line blank and listed supporting details below. The important part of this question is the blank line. I know I'm actually looking for a label that describes all of the examples. I'm pretty sure I know the answer now, but I'll look for confirming evidence in the text.

"Now that I know what questions I'll be asked, I can read and sift through paragraphs to find the answers. My purpose is set."

In addition to this sort of "solo" think-aloud, we often invite our students to think aloud along with us. During this kind of craft lesson, learners gather with the same released item and share how they make meaning, allowing peers to observe each other's processes. When we deepen the bench of teachers in our classrooms, we also deepen the collective well of knowledge.

It's important to remember that thinking aloud is about making our *in-the-head* work public. The purpose is broader than modeling how we "do the test." It's to offer insight about the thinking moves a test taker uses as she creates meaning.

We often end our think-alouds by asking students to share what they saw and heard. This reflection encourages students to name our thinking processes, instead of simply noticing surface behaviors.

COMPOSING—MANAGING CHALLENGING WORK FOR EXTENDED PERIODS OF TIME

The composing time is the longest part of the workshop, and that's intentional. Just as an apprentice would spend long periods of time emulating the skills of the mentor craftsman, students in classroom workshops need time to try out what they've learned. Composing is devoted to practice. It's hard to get better at golf if you never get the chance to play. The same is true for mathematicians, readers, writers, scientists, and historians. When students have the opportunity to work for thirty to fifty minutes each day problem-solving, experimenting, researching, drafting, and reading, their content expertise increases and so does their stamina.

This daily, extended work time also benefits our students as they grow in their capacity to take tests. Students who have developed the ability to endure and resist the temptation to quit in their daily classroom work will take this internal fortitude with them into testing situations.

Susan Logan, a lab classroom teacher and staff developer for the PEBC, once talked to a group of national visitors about the importance of students being able to work with a variety of genres.

> *We no longer have the option of teaching a nonfiction unit in November and a poetry unit in April. Students are expected to be the kind of flexible readers who can read a narrative passage on page one of their testing booklet, a graph on page three, and an excerpt from a science textbook on page five. Our instruction has to help students meet these expectations. Students need to be reading from a wide variety of genres across the year.*

Susan's advice was wise. And her classroom library reflected this advice. Baskets of poetry books, tubs of narrative and nonfiction texts, and stacks of magazines and newspapers invited her students to discover how to read these different genres. All workshops depend on this kind of variety.

Mathematicians rely on a variety of manipulatives and tools to work their way through problems. Scientists use assorted equipment to conduct experiments and multiple resources to do research. Historians require a range of text, visual data, and recordings to understand the significance of past events. And writers surround themselves with the kind of writing they want to produce. Without this diversity, students are less apt to learn to manage new and unfamiliar work.

For test takers, the opportunity to explore tools, different texts, problems, and situations allows them to face unfamiliar testing items. We can't know the exact stories they'll have to read, math problems they'll need to solve, or science topics they'll need to work through on any given standardized measure. But the variety we offer in our classroom workshops develops student flexibility and efficacy.

However, the power of a workshop structure goes beyond variety. It implies that students can access many layers of classroom support. Think-alouds provide metacognitive insight. Conferences focus on individuals' demonstrated needs and questions. Small-group instruction addresses the precise, identified needs of a few. Talk throughout a workshop encourages students to benefit from the knowledge of their peers. These key components create a safety net for students to explore many different levels of work.

For test takers, working through hard tests *with* the support of their teacher and classmates builds internal capacity to do the same sort of work in actual testing situations. Intentional classroom workshops are always full of chances to "muck about" with different materials and activities. Whether a tangled science research question, a multistep math problem, controversial historical issues, or a content-laden text, managing challenge becomes familiar and possible when learners know how to dig into difficult work.

We know from education experts that working in "just-right" books and activities is an important way for students to develop fluency and confidence. Spending too much time in challenging texts or overly difficult activities can lead to unnecessary frustration. However, if students don't experience texts that are beyond a comfortable reading level, if they aren't asked to have a go at complex math or confusing science, their willingness to hang with this kind of work goes undeveloped.

Experience teaches us to endure when the challenge is great. Our students ought to have the chance to know what it feels like to live beyond "just right" at times. They need to know we are confident that they can manage hard work. Composing time lets students build this same sort of confidence in themselves.

REFLECTING—BEING METACOGNITIVE

Every workshop ends with reflection. Students come together to share their growing understandings—about content, about strategies, about their own processes as learners. Teachers participate in this sharing, act as "data collectors" charting growth patterns, observe silently, or simply facilitate the talk. This is a time to render the day's thinking; a time for individual insights to bubble to the surface; a time to add to the growing collective wisdom; a time to elaborate on previous learning; a time to receive feedback and to contemplate future goals.

The purpose of reflecting is simple: to discuss emerging insights. The outcomes and structures of the reflecting session may vary from day to day, but this purpose is always the same.

As students uncover new insights about tests and their growing capacity to take tests, reflection becomes the forum for making those insights a part of the classroom community. The talk is more than "The answer to number three is B. Who got that right?" It's "How did you go about this part of the test? How did you keep yourself going when you got tired? How did you manage the tricky parts? What lessons will you take with you?"

With students gathered together, composing work in hand, we often launch into reflection by sharing an important aha gleaned from conferring:

"Guys, listen to Dominique explain what she figured out about how her own questions were different from the kinds of questions the test maker wrote."

Or

"When I was conferring with Molly, she shared her frustration about not being able to switch tests like she can switch topics when her writing is going nowhere. Molly, why don't you talk to the group about what you found yourself doing to dig back in?"

Sometimes, we might invite a single student or a small group of students to put their work on the overhead and talk about the thinking they jotted in the margins (see Figure 3.2).

Other times, we might ask everyone to turn "knee to knee" and talk with a partner or two about the ways they applied that day's craft lesson.

Figure 3.2. Three fourth graders, Emelia, Molly, and Emily, jot their shared thinking about these reading test questions on a transparency before sharing with their classmates.

Emelia Molly Emily

21 Why does Enrique write that this trip is the best thing that ever happened to him?

○ A He has dreamed of riding through the rain forest on a canopy tram.

○ B He had to work hard to write an essay about the rain forest.

○ C He has always wanted to take a trip with his parents.

○ D He has been interested in rain forests since he was a small child.

He came right out and told me "he has wanted to go to the rain forest since he was five".

22 From information in the selection, the reader can tell that the rain forest in Costa Rica is —

○ F a little-known vacation spot

○ G full of loud noises

○ H home to some unusual animals

○ J dangerous for humans

It doesn't come out and say it but he probably was intending unusual animals

23 Look at the following web of information from the selection.

Regardless of the format, reflecting at the end of each workshop gives our students the time to consider their thinking and to take a metacognitive stance toward their own growing understandings.

Unfortunately, reflecting is often the part of the workshop that gets "cut." Perhaps the bell is about to ring, perhaps the craft lesson went too long, perhaps time wasn't managed wisely. Reflecting is the time when teachers and students synthesize the day's work. It's too important to skip.

In his book *Reworking the Workshop*, Daniel Heuser (2002) says, "Having time for reflection is a shrinking commodity for children. Students in many classrooms are rushed from activity to activity, with little time to think about what they have done. It is little wonder that Nothing is the stock response to What did you do at school today?" (27).

Reflecting as a regular part of any classroom workshop provides students with the opportunity to develop perseverance and persistence of thought.

Imagine the increase in power of our students' thinking if they are simply given time to share their learning each day—even as test takers. As one of Patrick's students said recently, "I love when we come back to the floor to talk about our learning. It makes me realize that my learning *and* my thinking are important."

WHO DECIDES IN A WORKSHOP?
PURPOSE, OWNERSHIP, AND ACCOUNTABILITY

A few years ago, Cheryl observed Patrick teaching a questioning lesson. She was struck by a visual Patrick created with his third graders. The triangular chart represented their thinking about the origins of reading-related questions. Together, Patrick and his third graders noticed that sometimes the reader generated the questions, sometimes someone with whom the reader had a relationship (a teacher, a peer, a parent) generated the questions, and sometimes someone the reader did not know and was not ever likely to meet generated the questions. The nature of the questions, and of the answers, changed depending on the question source.

Patrick's original triangle graphic continues to evolve. The most current version is titled "Purpose" (see Figure 3.3). We've come to think of it as a way to represent the many decisions thinkers make, during school and across their lives. The graphic emphasizes the concepts of ownership (What am I doing?), purpose (Why am I doing this?), and accountability (To whom does this matter? Who is my audience? To whom am I accountable?). Sometimes the thinker gets to make all the decisions about ownership, purpose, and accountability. Sometimes someone with whom the thinker has a relationship makes the decisions. Sometimes the decision-making is a joint effort. And occasionally, someone the thinker does not know makes the decisions.

Figure 3.3

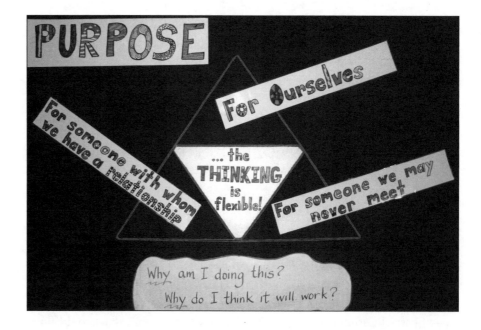

On a lazy Sunday afternoon, a reader might choose to read a tabloid magazine. She decides what to read and what to skip. She chooses her purpose for reading: to get the dirt on celebrity breakups. Whether or not she fulfills her purpose is up to her—she's accountable only to herself. She's operating in an "I decide" mode.

In contrast, to generate school improvement goals, a principal might ask teachers to analyze data reports. The teachers are operating in a "someone with whom I have a relationship decides" mode. Although the teachers are accountable to the principal, their working relationship allows for exploration, clarification, and negotiation as they go about completing the assigned task.

Now picture an eighth grader taking the state science test. The content has been chosen, the purpose decided. The eighth grader is accountable to a broad and largely unknown group of stakeholders. It's no secret that standardized testing presents unique demands. It falls into the category of "someone you don't know and will probably never meet decides." Unlike the case in class, at home, or on the soccer field, the student won't have the opportunity to explain or defend his thinking in person. He won't have the chance to sit alongside the test grader to explain the sound reasoning behind his answers. He has to climb inside the mind of the test maker to carefully choose and craft answers that will be judged proficient.

Our students deserve a wide variety of experiences in each of the three modes represented by the "Purpose" triangle. They deserve opportunities to choose their own writing topics, design their own science experiments, and create their own methods for deciding how much lumber to buy for the

Figure 3.4

Key A = Always S = Sometimes N = Not likely	For myself	For someone I know (teacher, parent, friend)	For someone I don't know (like CSAP)
I can choose what I want to read.	A	S	N
I can abandon my reading if I lose interest.	A	S	N
I can respond however I want.	A	S	N
I can explain my thinking verbally.	A	S	N
I can ask for help.	A	S	N
I can take as much time as I need.	A	S	N
I can work where ever I'm most comfortable.	A	S	N
I can use thinking strategies to help me understand.	A	A	A

backyard tree house. They also deserve to learn how to successfully meet and exceed the expectations of teachers, peers, family members, and future employers. And because testing is a reality in life, students deserve to be able to show what they know on standardized measures.

After working with the concept of purpose and who decides for many months, a group of third graders in Cheryl's class created a chart reflecting their understanding of different decision-making scenarios (see Figure 3.4). The chart shows that, through inquiry, explicit instruction, practice, and feedback, we can help our students develop a flexible and widely applicable understanding of ownership, purpose, and accountability.

THE CLASSROOM ENVIRONMENT REALLY DOES MATTER

After all is said and done, we believe that creating a thoughtful classroom workshop is just as important to students successfully navigating standardized tests as any of the instruction we might provide. The rituals and routines of a daily learning workshop

- clarify for students what might otherwise seem mysterious;
- offer students long periods of time to work independently without constant support or interruption;
- encourage students to manage "hard" texts and assignments;
- help students fine-tune their metacognition;
- invite students to explore the ways purpose, and who sets it, affects their precision.

Like any new skill, managing standardized tests demands ever-increasing stamina . . . stamina for working alone, stamina for tackling things that might be "out of level," stamina for pushing through boredom and distractions. By its very nature, a classroom workshop helps build this kind of stamina. Like speed or strength, stamina becomes something we can all get more of. And as Cheryl's students have so carefully articulated (see Figures 3.5 and 3.6), we can define it, measure it, monitor it, and put it to use when we need it most.

Figure 3.5

Choices that increase stamina ⬆	Choices that decrease stamina ⬇
• sitting in a place where I can focus	• sitting in a place where I'm distracted
• gathering the supplies I need	• being disorganized with supplies
• clarifying expectations and purpose	• confusing expectations and purpose
• monitoring the volume of my voice	• using a loud voice that distracts others
• selecting books/topics I'm interested in	• selecting books/topics I'm not interested in

Figure 3.6

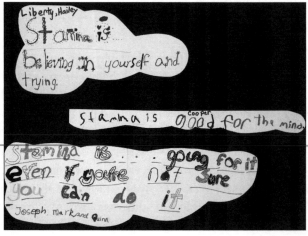

ONE ADDITIONAL THOUGHT

In his book *Testing Is Not Teaching*, Donald Graves reminds us of a pressing and often overlooked mission of education: to help students become long thinkers. Instead of focusing on only the "faster is better" mentality championed by virtually every timed standardized test, it's essential that we encourage students to engage in long thinking because it allows them to "pass from outside their subjects to the inside where they appreciate what it means to know" (Graves 2002, 54). For us, helping our students become long thinkers sits at the heart of our work with stamina.

Graves defines the characteristics often associated with long thinkers—characteristics we hope to foster in our students.

Long thinkers are problem finders.
They formulate their own questions about the world and then search for answers. Their search usually impels them to acquire a cluster of tools and skills that will help them achieve their goals.

Long thinkers enjoy their own company.
They are at home with their own thoughts and do not often require the company of others to pursue their goals. They will often pull out of a group to be alone with their thoughts. They are not necessarily antisocial, but they do require time alone.

Long thinkers have a sense of play.
In the midst of work they find play, a new way, a novel twist. This sense of play and discovery sustains their long thinking.

Long thinkers are highly focused.
They are able to sustain thought on one project to the exclusion of all else. They get caught up in their obsessions and special interests: learning to play an instrument or a piece of music, painting a scene, constructing a mechanism, reading a book, writing a book. They are often unaware of the passing of time.

Long thinkers have been apprenticed to other long thinkers.
They may be fortunate to have a parent, relative, or close friend who is a long thinker and so have witnessed the power of long thinking. Or they may have served a more formal apprenticeship. They may be fortunate enough to have a teacher who is a long thinker and consciously demonstrates long thinking through her own specialized interests, allowing the class to travel with her through the process. (54–55)

Thinking About Tests

INTRODUCTION: APPLYING PROFICIENT READER RESEARCH TO TEST TAKING

Comprehension is messy. There is no clear-cut path that the brain takes when making sense. There are many roads the mind can travel as it burrows through layer after layer of meaning. Good readers [learners] don't read every document, book, or magazine article the same way. They are aware of their thinking and consciously apply reading strategies that will help them cope with the demands of the task.

CRIS TOVANI

◆

Whether on the soccer field, the dance floor, or in the band room, children learn to name their moves. The soccer player heads the ball. The ballet dancer turns a pirouette. The trumpeter practices major and minor scales. Diligent coaches spend countless hours demonstrating moves and offering feedback.

"When your opponent kicks a high ball, block it with a header."

"The competition judges are looking for double pirouettes. Be sure to land in fifth position."

"Remember, in these measures the trumpet is supposed to simulate an echo. You've got to create a softer, more faraway tone to your notes."

Eventually, coaches are relegated to the sidelines. The young players take the stage—aware, strategic, and poised for success.

The thinking strategy research led us to value the practice of naming cognitive moves in the field of academics. We helped student mathematicians see that when they eyeballed the length of a line, they were estimating—a very smart strategy akin to inferring. When young writers described seashells in vivid detail, we helped them notice how they had created mental images for their audience.

We believed in helping students name their moves as readers, writers, mathematicians, historians, and scientists. With this help, our students' awareness increased, leading them to greater learning success.

So why not help our students name their cognitive moves as test takers?

In Chapter 1, we shared our own stories of taking standardized tests. We gathered released items, sequestered ourselves in a quiet room, and walked the walk of test takers. Because our primary purpose was to gain insight into the moves we made as proficient (we hoped!) test takers, we jotted in the margins as we worked from initial directions to final answers, then backtracked to compare the thinking spurred by particular question formats, key words, and graphic organizers.

After much practice and discourse, we were sure we could help our students do the same thing.

We found our missing link.

We realized that helping learners discover the relationship between the work they do in our classrooms on a daily basis and the work they do only six to nine days a year would make the chore of testing less burdensome; rather than *teach to* the test we could help students *think to* the test.

We also realized that by connecting the bigger picture of learning—the metacognitive element—to test taking we'd relieve some of the stress we all felt bubbling to the surface, regardless of our agreement or disagreement with the notion of high-stakes tests.

Asking questions, creating mental images, drawing inferences, synthesizing new ideas, activating schema, determining what's important, monitoring meaning, and problem-solving when meaning breaks down all help test takers understand test content: stories, poems, articles, expository passages, word problems, and graphics embedded in any standardized test. And knowing how to use these same strategies helps test takers navigate the demands posed by high-stakes achievement measures.

If we, as teachers, nudge students to apply these strategies naturally to testing situations, they'll think more clearly, confidently, and concisely.

Our goal, ultimately, is to teach learners to think. Thinking and learning are synonymous—and test taking has become a part of our ongoing classroom discourse with learners.

A CAUTION . . .

As we plan a strategy study for our students, we're careful to include as many contexts and applications as possible, stretching across various content areas, various genres, and various instructional settings. The vignettes and craft lessons we've written about exemplify the kind of talk and explicit teaching we structure for our students. But in the same way we wouldn't narrow our reading to only nonfiction for weeks on end or spend day after day memorizing only math facts, we'd never focus solely on tests for days and days. We strive to make our instruction a bit more subtle, a bit more interwoven, a bit more seamless.

Linking strategy work to standardized tests inside a broader study gives us the opportunity to teach students to think *through* them. We know we have to make it a part of the strategy work we value. This way, thinking through tests becomes valuable, worthy work for students . . . but not the only work they do.

Chapter 4
TEST TAKERS Ask Questions

Every day we ask hundreds of questions. We watch the weather forecast on the morning news and wonder, "What outfit should I wear today?" We double-check with a spouse: "Are you picking up the kids after school or am I?" We approach a teammate for suggestions: "How are you going to introduce equivalent fractions to your students?" Our questions create clarity and purpose in our lives.

The scientific method—posing a question, creating a hypothesis, gathering data, arriving at a conclusion—is the accepted protocol for confirming, expanding, and revising what we've come to know about our world. A scientist's questions might challenge the accuracy of a colleague's research report or create new direction for a study she's spent her career exploring. Curiosity drives scientists toward new understandings and new endeavors.

As test takers, our questions often clarify the requirements of a testing situation. Because a test's purpose and audience pose narrow guidelines, questions can help determine how to respond to a testing item. Knowing a test's purpose ensures that what we provide for evaluators is a true demonstration of what we know and are able to do.

Test takers . . .

- ensure they understand the expectations of each test question. ("The question talks about archaeologists and finding buried items on a coordinate grid. Do they want me to plot points or decide which items are at certain points?")
- identify the kind of questions a test includes. ("Is this an in-the-text kind of question, where the answer is stated directly in the passage? Or is this an on–my-own kind of question that I'll need to make an inference about?" Raphael 1986)

- clarify the specific test or test item's format. ("Is this a multiple-choice test where I can scan the passage for correct answers, or am I going to need to read closely so I can create a well-developed constructed response?")
- determine the content knowledge being assessed. ("The picture shows stair steps that need to be built with concrete. Will I need to use the given dimensions to find area or volume?")

Student Examples—Naming What They Notice About Tests and Asking Questions

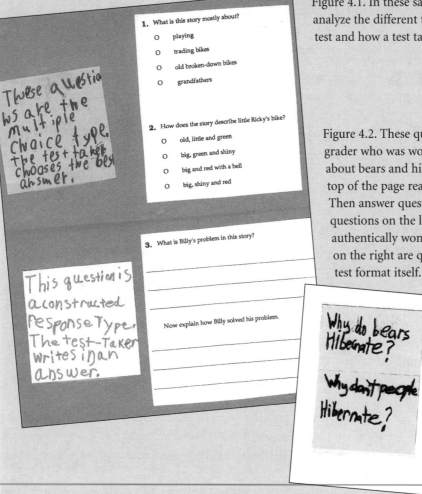

Figure 4.1. In these samples, Cheryl's third graders analyze the different types of questions they find on a test and how a test taker needs to respond to each.

Figure 4.2. These questions are from Amelia, a third grader who was working on a sample test passage about bears and hibernation. The directions at the top of the page read, "Read this article about bears. Then answer questions 6 through 12." The questions on the left are the things Amelia authentically wonders about hibernation. Those on the right are questions she asks because of the test format itself.

Student Examples—Naming What They Notice About Tests and Asking Questions

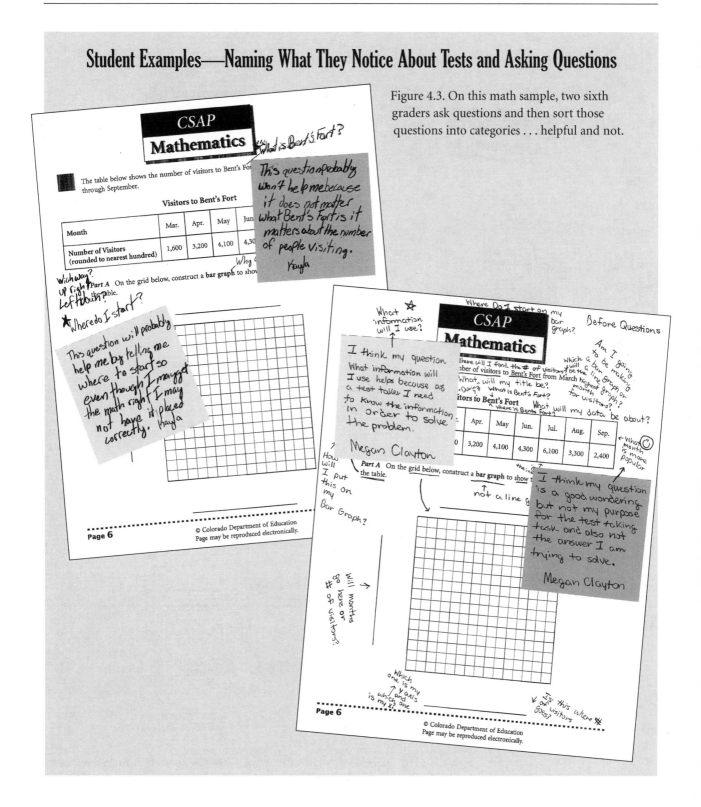

Figure 4.3. On this math sample, two sixth graders ask questions and then sort those questions into categories . . . helpful and not.

Student Examples—Naming What They Notice About Tests and Asking Questions

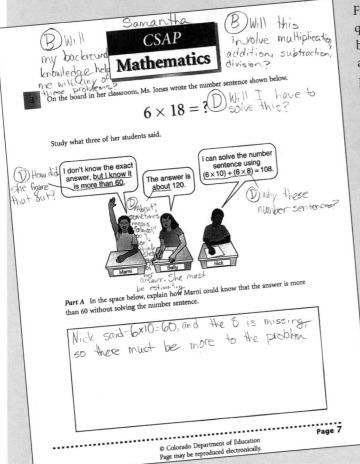

Figure 4.4. Here, Samantha registers the questions she asks (coded with a circled B) before she begins taking the practice test as well as those she asks while working through the problems (coded with a circled D).

STORIES FROM THE CLASSROOM

Comparing Our Questions to the Test Makers'—A Lesson with Fourth Graders

By Lori L. Conrad

It was evident to any visitor what sort of work the fourth graders had been doing for the past couple of weeks. Charts outlining the power of asking questions lined the walls. Everything—from "Questions Writers Ask Themselves" to quotes about the power of using questioning as a tool for thinking to three triangles showing how questions can occur before/during/after we read, can be about words/sentences/ideas, and can be answered by the text/by our schema/by inferring—recorded the kind of in-depth thinking the students had already done.

So when I asked them to "catch me up" on their study, insights tumbled out.

"There should be a little voice in your head asking questions," Molly began. "You need to be aware of them because they help you understand. The more you know, the more information you have, the more important your questions become."

"Yeah, if you don't have any questions, you're probably not paying attention to your reading," Maureen added.

"I notice my questions right away. Sometimes they help me figure out what I don't get, and sometimes they make me want to read more," Emelia shared.

"It's like you ask a question, keep reading, find an answer, know you're getting it," Drew said.

Patrick's hand waved for attention. "But the answers don't always come from the story. There are different places we can find answers."

"And sometimes you have to ignore a question because it doesn't really matter much, and if you pay too much attention to it, you get sort of stuck," Emily added.

It was clear they'd done a lot of thinking about the ways generating their own questions supported learners' meaning making. They were living out the research so often cited about the power of students taking an active role in questioning the books they read, the problems they solve, the writing they compose. But how would all this work compare with the job of answering the kind of questions test makers generate?

"You've done some impressive thinking," I said. "You all have figured out a lot over the last few weeks. But here's what I need you to help me think through. How do the questions you ask yourself as you work to make sense of a piece of text compare with the kinds of questions you'd encounter on a test? Go grab a clipboard, four sticky notes, and your pencil, and join me back up here on the floor."

As the kids gathered what they needed from their desks, I took out a released item from Massachusetts's fourth-grade English Language Arts state test. It contained three pages from Kate DiCamillo's book *Because of Winn-Dixie*.

"Put your four stickies on the clipboard so you can see all of them at once. I'm going to read this story excerpt to you, stopping four times. Each time I stop, jot down what you're wondering about. I'll do the same on the chart paper here."

As I read through the passage that introduces the mangy Winn-Dixie to India Opal's preacher father, the fourth graders noted the questions they had. Some of the questions they recorded on the stickies named confusions: "What does an exception mean?" (Kellen); "What does it mean to be a suffering dog?" (Emelia); "How could Winn-Dixie really understand Opal? He's a dog!" (Tanner).

Some of their questions helped them figure out the characters and the story's problem: "I wonder why the dog is homeless. He seems so nice" (Nicole); "Why did the preacher give in so easily? Why was being less fortunate so important to both him and Opal?" (Kamren); "Does she [Opal] like being a preacher's kid? Would I?" (Tucker).

And still other questions pushed them to think forward into the story: "How is the trailer park owner going to react to Winn-Dixie?" (Kilian); "I wonder if the preacher falls in love with Winn-Dixie like Opal has?" (Carsyn).

"Now I want you and a partner to take your own copy of the story and give it a second read," I said. "When you're finished, go ahead and think through the questions the test makers have written. You can answer them if you want, but what I'm really interested in is how you think these questions compare with the ones we've just asked on our own. When we come back to the carpet, that's what I'll want you to share."

As the students scattered to quiet spots in the room, Angel and I gave them a few minutes to reread the excerpt before beginning to confer.

"Tucker, what have you figured out?"

He looked up at me with knowing blue eyes. "The questions that the test maker writes are only about the story. They're based on the story. I use my own thinking when I ask questions."

"Say more about that. What do you mean exactly?"

"Well, when I asked, 'Does she like being a preacher's kid?' it was because I really wanted to figure that out, to think about it. The test makers' questions are about their thinking and what they want me to understand. That's why they give me answers to choose from. It's their thinking."

Kellen nodded in affirmation. "They tell us the questions instead of us asking them. I have to do some different thinking. When I answer the test, I have to think about what the question is asking. When I ask my own questions, I have to think about what the story is saying."

I moved on to Olivia, Dominique, and Maureen.

"I figured something out," Olivia volunteered. "The questions I sometimes ask make me want to read more. But I don't have to read on to figure out the questions a test person asks. These questions don't make us think forward. You can just look back in the story."

"Yeah, these questions are in the past of the book," Maureen added.

This insight made me look up from my notes. "What do you mean?"

"Well, when I asked, 'Will the preacher let her keep Winn-Dixie?' I really wanted to read on to find out what happened," Dominique said. "The questions the test maker wrote don't make me want to do that."

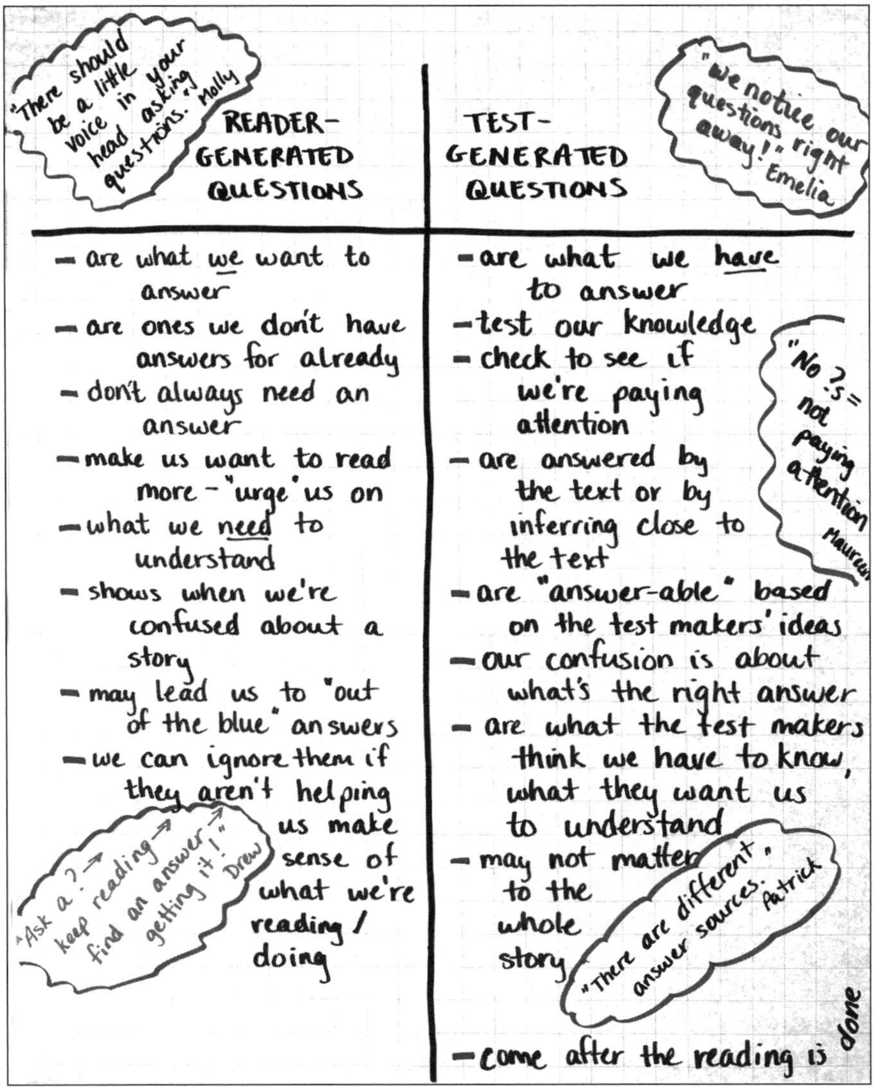

Figure 4.5

Figure 4.5 — T chart: "Reader-Generated Questions" and "Test-Generated Questions"

READER-GENERATED QUESTIONS

"There should be a little voice in your head asking questions." Molly

- are what we want to answer
- are ones we don't have answers for already
- don't always need an answer
- make us want to read more – "urge" us on
- what we need to understand
- shows when we're confused about a story
- may lead us to "out of the blue" answers
- we can ignore them if they aren't helping us make sense of what we're reading / doing

"Ask a ? → keep reading → find an answer!" Drew getting it!

TEST-GENERATED QUESTIONS

"We notice our questions right away!" Emelia

- are what we have to answer
- test our knowledge
- check to see if we're paying attention
- are answered by the text or by inferring close to the text
- are "answer-able" based on the test makers' ideas
- our confusion is about what's the right answer
- are what the test makers think we have to know, what they want us to understand
- may not matter to the whole story
- come after the reading is done

"No ?s = not paying attention" Maureen

"There are different answer sources." Patrick

"So, your questions often give you a purpose for reading, but the test questions really don't." The three girls nodded and I moved on.

When the class returned to the carpet, they couldn't wait to share their new insights. We created a T chart based on their ideas (Figure 4.5).

By thinking about the act of questioning as both something we do for ourselves and something others might do to check to see if we're "paying attention," the fourth graders were able to come to powerful generalizations that should make asking their own questions and answering someone else's easier to do. It also helped Angel and me demystify tests just a bit.

Asking Questions Before, During, and After—Thinking Through Sixth-Grade Mathematics Together

By Patrick A. Allen

As I walked into Ms. Manzanares's classroom, I recognized many of the students' faces. Some of the faces were those of my former students. As I glanced around the room, I noticed the same gleam of curiosity in their eyes that I had seen back when they were third graders, only now with a more defined sense of maturity. As I asked them to gather around, I heard Justin say, "It's just like the good old days."

I said to myself, "Yep, same old kids." Although I did not know all the faces, there was a tone of familiarity when I asked the simple question, "Who can tell me about the strategies you use as learners?" Hands shot up. Voices filled the air. The room was abuzz with the language of strategies.

After spending a few minutes connecting and reconnecting, I wrote a simple question on the chart: "How does asking questions help a test taker?" I turned to the students and said, "This is what we're going to figure out. How *does* asking questions help a test taker?" Then I wrote the words *before, during,* and *after* under the question. "And this is how we'll organize our thinking today—on the *before* questions we ask as test takers, on the *during* questions that arise as we work, and finally on the *after* questions that linger once we're finished. Sound familiar?" Many heads nodded—familiar strategy, different context.

"First, you're going to watch as I think aloud to demonstrate my thinking." I placed a released math item dealing with profit and data analysis on the document camera. "Your job is to listen to my thinking. I'm going to be jotting down my questions as I work through the problem, even though we know we can't do that when we're really taking a test, right? I want you to take note of what I'm doing and we'll chat about that when I'm finished."

I began thinking through the paragraph and shared my initial questions: "Will this be about money?" "Will all three parts of the problem fit together?" "Have I seen this before?" "Will I have to fill in a graph?" I commented, "I notice my questions are helping me clarify my purpose, but I'm not really looking for an answer at this point. And trust me, it's been a long time since I've attempted a problem like this one."

I began to read the problem and notice my questions. Immediately I asked about the graph ("What are these lines for?" "How do I read this?"), the directions and sentence statements ("What is a profit?" "Why are there three parts?"), and the mathematics itself ("Is there a pattern?" "Why are these numbers arranged this way?"). Thinking aloud provided the framework to guide students to work on another piece I had chosen for them to use. I spent about ten minutes modeling and jotting down my thinking.

I finished my think-aloud with one *after* question: "Did I do everything?" Because I wanted students to have a go independently, I stopped after Part B of the three-part problem. "What did you notice me doing as a test taker?" I asked. I jotted down their answers on a sticky note (see Figure 4.6).

"You guys noticed a lot, and this should help us add some great thinking to our chart at the end of our workshop. Some of the things you noticed might help answer our question, 'How does asking questions help a test taker?' Are you ready to have a go with this on your own?" The kids were eager to get started.

Before I sent them off to work, I said, "On the back of each of your papers, I've placed three sticky notes. Those are for you to jot down any thinking you might have about how asking a specific question helped you as a test taker. Let me show you what I mean. When I asked the question, 'What are these lines for?' that really helped me look for the key box. It clarified for me that the solid line on the graph showed the profit for sweaters and the dashed line showed the profit for pairs of jeans. If I hadn't asked that question, I don't think I would have even noticed the key—and I needed it to answer Part A on the problem. So, that's how my question helped me." I wrote it on a sticky note and stuck it on the graph on my paper.

> What We Noticed...
>
> - You asked more questions "during" than you did "before."
> - You answered your questions while you were working.
> - You picked just the most important questions that popped in your head.
> - You underlined and paid attention to key words and phrases.
> - You asked if it would be smart to show two ways to solve a problem in the box.
> - You looked back at the graph and asked questions.
> - You made sure you answered all the parts of the question.
> - You always asked "Does this make sense?"
> - You had more questions than answers—that was a good thing.

Figure 4.6

I handed out a problem and students found a comfortable spot in the room to work. I reminded them, "Remember, we're not necessarily worried about solving the problem; we're really going to focus on the questions that are rumbling through our heads." As students worked, I conferred.

I sat down next to Maille. "Maille, what are you noticing?"

She looked up and smiled. "Some of my questions have lots of parts and some don't have as many parts."

"Tell me more." I was hoping for some clarification.

"If I ask questions before I get started, I can be prepared if there's multiplication or something. If I get it right because I've asked a good question, I'm better prepared. The parts fit together."

"Hmm . . . So how do you think asking questions might be helping?"

"It helps me with getting the answer . . . I can think through the problem before I do it." She noticed that she was thinking *through* rather than plowing through. I let her work and continued on with several other students.

I sat down next to Richy. "What are you thinking about?"

"I'm just wondering if I'll do good or bad. That's what I think about all the time. If I don't ask questions, I might not succeed. I kinda worry. At the same time I know I'm going to do well."

"It sounds to me, Richy, like tests worry you a lot. Today just have some fun. Try your best. Think about the questions you're asking that might help you."

Before I sat down with another student, I noted Richy's concerns to share with Ms. Manzanares later. Then I moved on to Taylor.

"How's it going, Taylor?" I asked, and I waited.

She looked up at me. "I'm thinking of multiplication problems I know that have answers higher than sixty. I'm asking myself what they are . . . Then, when I started looking at these drawings, I got lots of questions. Do *they* [the students in the drawing] have the exact answer? That's what I'm asking." (See Figure 4.7.)

"You're off to a good start. What else are you thinking?"

"Well, by studying the drawings carefully, it helped me eliminate some of the questions I was asking."

"How did eliminating questions help you?" I was intrigued.

"I can focus more on questions I don't know the answers to . . . I can focus on the math. Then I wonder if I've explained enough and ask myself, Have I explained enough? That's what I'm thinking so far about how questions help me."

"It sounds like you're really thinking about this notion of questioning. I'll let you work." I continued to let the students work independently.

After twenty minutes of independent work, I announced, "Kids, before you come down to chat, please try to have at least one sticky note that explains how a question helped you as a test taker. Be ready to share when we come back together in three minutes." I glanced at the clock and knew we had ten minutes left to reflect.

I went back to our original question. As students gathered, I said, "What did you discover?"

Figure 4.7

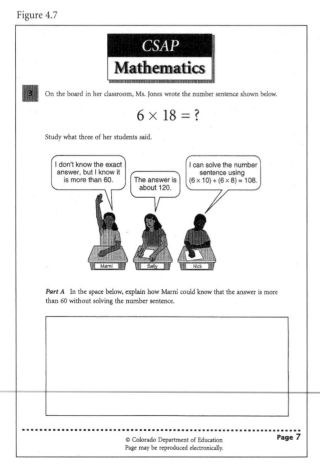

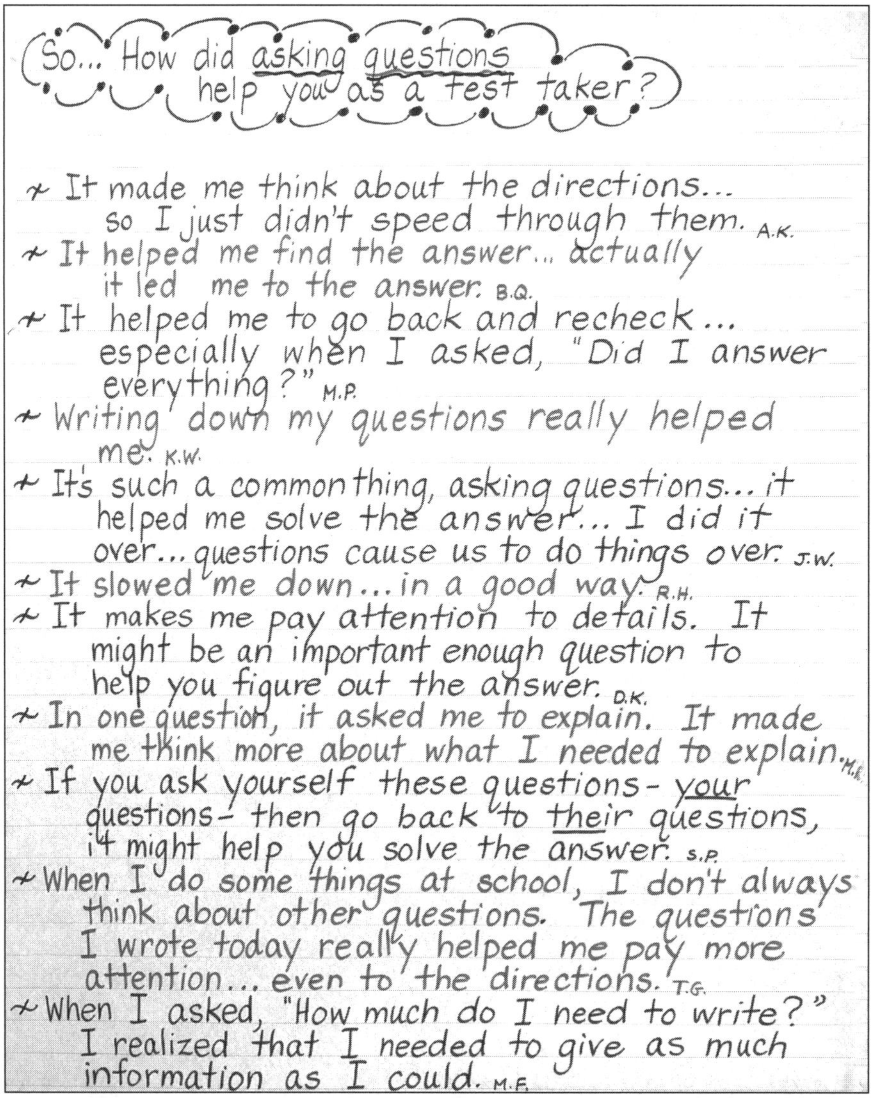
So... How did asking questions help you as a test taker?

- It made me think about the directions... so I just didn't speed through them. A.K.
- It helped me find the answer... actually it led me to the answer. B.Q.
- It helped me to go back and recheck... especially when I asked, "Did I answer everything?" M.P.
- Writing down my questions really helped me. K.W.
- It's such a common thing, asking questions... it helped me solve the answer... I did it over... questions cause us to do things over. J.W.
- It slowed me down... in a good way. R.H.
- It makes me pay attention to details. It might be an important enough question to help you figure out the answer. D.K.
- In one question, it asked me to explain. It made me think more about what I needed to explain.
- If you ask yourself these questions - your questions - then go back to their questions, it might help you solve the answer. S.P.
- When I do some things at school, I don't always think about other questions. The questions I wrote today really helped me pay more attention... even to the directions. T.G.
- When I asked, "How much do I need to write?" I realized that I needed to give as much information as I could. M.F.

Figure 4.8

They shared their responses as I recorded them on a chart (see Figure 4.8).

Many students said asking questions simply helped them slow down and not rush. They captured the very essence of questioning. Paying attention to the questions they asked before, during, and after allowed students to begin to slow down their thinking to deal with the complexities involved in problem-solving. This provided them with the opportunity to work through the problem at a comfortable pace. It gave them thinking time. The familiarity with the strategy of questioning seemed to bring a sense of clarity to their work.

POSSIBILITIES: Craft Lessons for Asking Questions

What kinds of test questions can we expect?
> Notice patterns across several sample tests to discover the range of questions. (E.g., in most reading tests, there's a *main idea* question and a *vocabulary* question.)

How does the way a test question is framed affect how we go about determining the answer?
> Name the question's structure and how it affects the answer's complexity. (E.g., multiple-choice questions, constructed-response prompts, multiple-part questions.)

What questions might we ask ourselves as we negotiate a test?
> List the self-generated, clarifying questions a test taker asks while navigating a testing situation. (E.g., "How much time do I have?" "Can I guess and not be penalized?" "How am I supposed to show what I know?" "Did I meet the requirements?")

How do test questions focus our attention on essential elements of a problem or passage?
> Discover how test questions act as a compass *pointing the way* to what a test taker needs to bring into focus. (E.g., "In the graph below, what three things are being compared?")

How would we use questioning to make sense of this material if we found it outside of a testing situation?
> Ask specific questions to enhance understanding of test content. (E.g., "How would I punctuate a sentence that includes a series of examples?" "How do I reduce fractions?" "How do crystals form?")

Chapter 5
TEST TAKERS Create Mental Images

Do you remember the smell of cookies baking in your grandmother's kitchen? Does the sound of church bells ringing on a Sunday morning take you back to a certain place and time? What about the taste of a favorite dish from a special restaurant that, no matter how hard you try to replicate the recipe at home, never tastes as good?

When we read poems like Billy Collins's "A Portrait of the Reader with a Bowl of Cereal," we can't help but *see* the "curve of the blue and white pitcher, the tea leaves of some dream stuck to the china slope of the hour." We can't help but *hear* the door swing open or *feel* the morning air. Talented poets, and the wonderful poetry they write, make this possible. And these same sorts of images flash across our minds when we read a great novel or a well-crafted entry in a scientific journal.

But how do these mental images help test takers answer items designed to measure their capacity to solve a geometry problem or understand an expository piece about whales?

Mental images—the sights, sounds, smells, tastes, tactile feelings, and emotions thinkers create as they make sense of their world—help test takers understand test content and envision their answers and products.

A test taker will . . .

- envision the work required by a test item. ("The directions give me four points to include when writing the answer. I'll need to double-check when I've finished drafting to be sure I've included all four.")
- use graphic models that tests provide. ("The test includes this graphic organizer I'm supposed to use to record my answer and there's this empty space, too. I'll need to show my initial work in the blank space and then put my final answer in the organizer at the bottom of the page.")

- create a cognitive map of the testing materials so she can think back to specific portions of the test while answering questions. ("Oh, that phrase must have been at the top of the second page where the main character was talking.")
- create an image in the test evaluator's mind about who he is and what he knows. ("If I use this sort of language in my response, the evaluator will see what I know and how I think as a scientist." "I want my penmanship to be easy to read because it's a visual statement about me.")

Student Examples—Naming What They Notice About Tests and Creating Mental Images

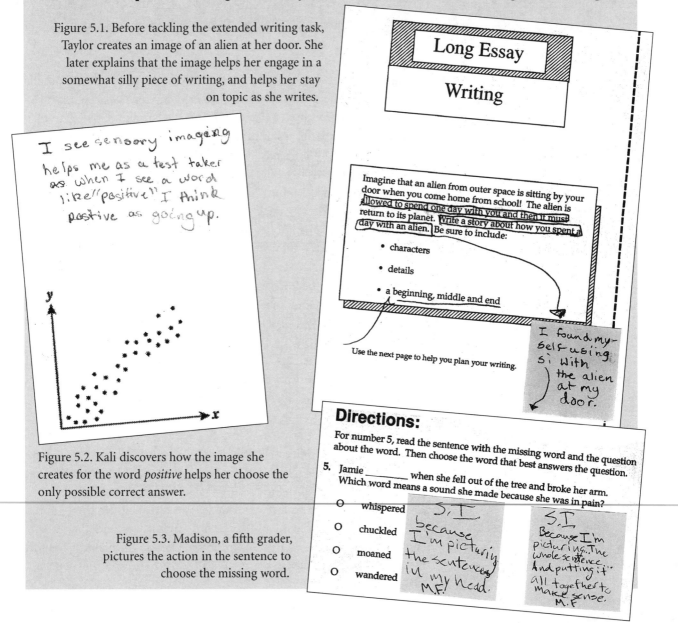

Figure 5.1. Before tackling the extended writing task, Taylor creates an image of an alien at her door. She later explains that the image helps her engage in a somewhat silly piece of writing, and helps her stay on topic as she writes.

Figure 5.2. Kali discovers how the image she creates for the word *positive* helps her choose the only possible correct answer.

Figure 5.3. Madison, a fifth grader, pictures the action in the sentence to choose the missing word.

Student Examples—Naming What They Notice About Tests and Creating Mental Images

Figure 5.4. In these samples from a third-grade math test, Samantha and Mackenzie both name the ways they picture math work in their minds. Whether counting or recreating a math strategy, having a visual image supports their mathematical meaning making.

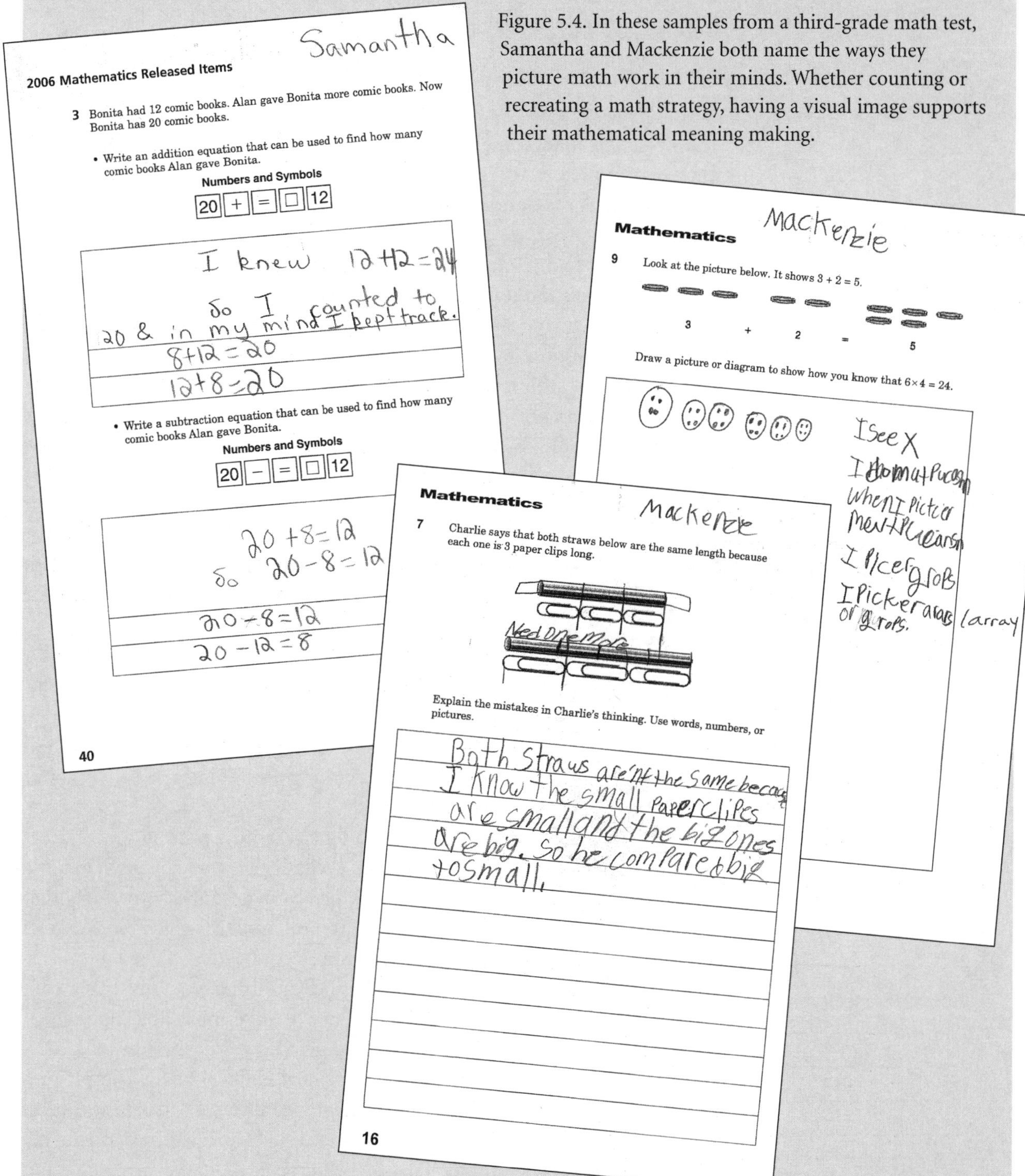

Samantha

2006 Mathematics Released Items

3 Bonita had 12 comic books. Alan gave Bonita more comic books. Now Bonita has 20 comic books.

- Write an addition equation that can be used to find how many comic books Alan gave Bonita.

Numbers and Symbols

20 + = □ 12

I knew 12+12=24
so I counted to
20 & in my mind I kept track.
8+12=20
12+8=20

- Write a subtraction equation that can be used to find how many comic books Alan gave Bonita.

Numbers and Symbols

20 − = □ 12

20+8=12
so 20−8=12
20−8=12
20−12=8

40

Mathematics   **Mackenzie**

9 Look at the picture below. It shows 3 + 2 = 5.

3   +   2   =   5

Draw a picture or diagram to show how you know that 6×4 = 24.

I see X
I do mat Pic on
when I Pic or
ment Pic or arons
I Plcer groB
I Pick er arons I array
or groBs.

Mathematics   **Mackenzie**

7 Charlie says that both straws below are the same length because each one is 3 paper clips long.

Ned one More

Explain the mistakes in Charlie's thinking. Use words, numbers, or pictures.

Both straws aren't the same because
I know the small paperclips
are small and the big ones
are big. so he compared big
to small.

16

STORIES FROM THE CLASSROOM

Do Mental Images Play a Role in Success on a Writing Test?

By Cheryl Zimmerman

Testing season had come and gone in third grade. But on a sunny May morning, our study of the connection between thinking strategies and success on tests continued as we gathered for our writing craft lesson.

"Across the year, we've been exploring the ways thinking strategies help us take tests," I said. "Today I'm wondering specifically about mental images, and I have a question for you. Do you think it helps to create mental images while taking a writing test? Think about that for a minute." I paused to think through the question myself. "Now, turn and talk with someone next to you. Share your initial thinking about my question."

Third graders turned knee to knee with partners. I knelt next to Alyssa and Alex. "I don't know, actually. I think of creating images when I'm writing poetry," Alyssa explained to Alex. "If the test makers ask us to write poetry, then mental images might help."

"I agree," said Alex. "I'm thinking any kind of writing is better when the writer creates images for the reader."

After listening in on a few other conversations, I asked the students to pivot back toward me. "Now that you've had a chance to share with your partner, let's take a look at some of the items we might encounter on a writing test. Think specifically about mental images."

I displayed a typical writing prompt on the overhead projector: "What makes you happy? Write a paragraph in which you describe something that makes you happy and explain **why** it makes you happy." (See Figure 5.5.)

"Hmm. What do you think, you guys? What are you thinking about this prompt and the use of mental images?"

Cearra raised her hand. "The prompt says *describe*. In order to describe, I'd create a mental image. I'd see what makes me happy flash in my mind. I'd use that image to make my paragraph better. Like I might write about my new puppy. I can

Figure 5.5

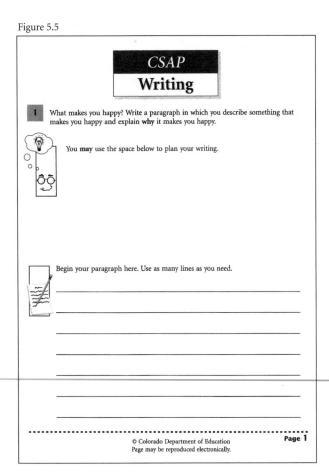

CSAP
Writing

1   What makes you happy? Write a paragraph in which you describe something that makes you happy and explain **why** it makes you happy.

You **may** use the space below to plan your writing.

Begin your paragraph here. Use as many lines as you need.

© Colorado Department of Education   **Page 1**
Page may be reproduced electronically.

picture the way she just sits there when I try to walk her on a leash, and how that makes me and my mom giggle."

Blythe chimed in next. "We talk about putting voice into our writing so that it's memorable for our readers. It's the same with a writing test prompt. Voice helps a reader create images. It's probably important to help the test graders create images if we want them to know we're good writers."

"I'm thinking that's true, Blythe. We've noticed that we're drawn to writers who use precise language because that language helps us create images, which in turn help us understand and remember what we read. If we want test graders to understand and remember our writing, we'll want to use image-rich language when responding to a prompt.

"Let's keep thinking about that, and now let's look at another kind of item we might see on a writing test." I displayed another test sample (see Figure 5.6), an editing test item consisting of a paragraph with underlined words and phrases. The directions say that each underlined word or phrase *may* contain an error in grammar and usage, punctuation, capitalization, or spelling. "What about this? Any chance that creating images will help a test taker on this sort of item? Samantha, what are you thinking?"

"It's not like the prompt. This paragraph is already written."

"True. So if something is already written and you're playing the role of editor, do mental images help in any way?" I scanned the class. Michael's hand shot up. "Michael?"

"See where the phrase *United states* is underlined? I get a sense that something is wrong there because I can picture how those two words are supposed to look. The *s* on *states* is supposed to be capitalized. I didn't really have to create that image—it was already in my mind. I guess I used an image I already had in my brain."

"So maybe on an item like this you use the images you've collected in your mind instead of creating new ones. Is that what you're thinking, Michael?"

"Yeah. Look at the underlined word *to*. Same thing. I know it's supposed to mean the number two, and I have an image of how that's spelled. They made a mistake."

"I agree with Michael's thinking," said Cearra. "When you're editing, you keep your eye out for things that look funny; things that don't match the images you have in your head."

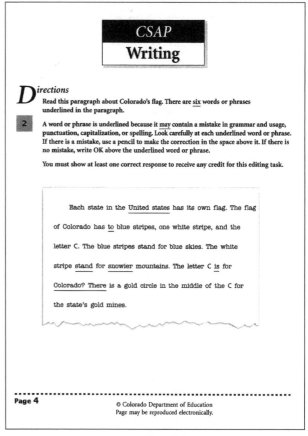

Figure 5.6

Directions:

For numbers 1 to 6, choose the sentence that shows the <u>correct</u> capitalization and punctuation.

1.
   - O Have you ever been to the hot springs in glenwood springs.
   - O Have you ever been to the hot springs in Glenwood Springs?
   - O have you ever been to the hot springs in Glenwood Springs.
   - O Have you ever been to the hot springs in Glenwood springs?

2.
   - O Josh has a dog named Max.
   - O Josh has a Dog named Max.
   - O josh has a dog named Max?
   - O Josh has a dog named max?

3.
   - O My favorite Month of the year is December?
   - O My favorite month of the Year is December?
   - O My favorite Month of the Year is December.
   - O My favorite month of the year is December.

4.
   - O Kim yang can draw beautiful horses.
   - O She learned how to draw horses when she was six.
   - O Her drawings have won awards in art contests
   - O miss Yang lives in Pueblo, Colorado.

5.
   - O Latisha wants to be a Doctor when she grows up?
   - O She works hard in School so she can go to a good college
   - O Latisha hopes to attend denver University.
   - O Her mom is saving money for college.

6.
   - O Jose likes to eat dinner at Taco Bell
   - O His dad takes him to taco bell after piano lessons on Tuesdays.
   - O He orders a burrito, a taco, and a drink.
   - O jose likes lots of salsa on his burrito.

32

Figure 5.7

"Hold that thought, Cearra, and look at this one last page [see Figure 5.7]. These are the kinds of test questions that show four nearly identical sentences. The test taker is required to choose the sentence that shows the correct capitalization and punctuation. I'm thinking that what you just said applies to this, too."

"I think it does. When a sentence doesn't start with a capital letter, it doesn't match my image of how it's supposed to look. So I could eliminate the third choice on number one right away."

"And look at number three," Michael said, smiling. "That question mark looks funny at the end of the first choice because the sentence isn't a question. I could eliminate that choice too."

"I think you guys are definitely on to something here," I said. "Creating mental images, and using the images you have tucked away in your mind, might play a very important role in success on a writing test. Tomorrow we'll continue to think about this. Be ready to try some writing test items and we'll see what we discover."

The third-grade writers settled in with their current writing projects, and I took a moment to jot down some of their thoughts about the use of mental images on writing tests. As always, their thinking paved the way for future craft lessons.

Do Mathematicians Taking a Test Really Create Pictures in Their Heads? Figuring It Out with Third Graders

By Lori L. Conrad

"I heard that you guys have been busily studying the ways mathematicians create mental images as they work through math problems."

Hands filled the air as Sarah Grubb's third graders nodded vigorously.

"With geometry shapes. We have to create an image of what each one looks like to figure out the sides and angles," James began.

"We have to picture what the problem looks like . . . shapes or numbers," Max added.

"When we're writing in our notebook, we can't always see the whole shape—you know, if it's 3-D or something—so we have to imagine what the other sides look like in our heads," Seth commented.

"When you solve a math problem, you have the numbers in your head. You know, when we do mental math. You have to see what the problem is talking about in your head because you can't write it down," Amelia shared.

"Sometimes when we're doing a really hard math problem and we have to use manipulatives to figure it out, that's a mental image because we feel it and see it as we move the cubes or counters around," Cearra said.

As I tried to capture all this smart thinking on a piece of chart paper, I realized that the lesson I had planned for that day needed to be revised. I had hoped some of the insights Sarah's students were sharing would develop *as a result of* working through the released items I'd brought with me. Now my teaching had to take a different, more sophisticated path.

"Okay, it's pretty obvious that you guys really get this. You've already figured out so much! So what I'm left wondering is whether or not any of this changes if the math you're working on happens to be on a standardized test."

The students all sat quietly, thinking about this new wrinkle. I knew they'd had many opportunities across the year to explore released test items. Sarah shared these students with Cheryl, so using test samples periodically in their teaching was a routine they'd established early in the school year. And I knew the students were very experienced at keeping track of both their math answers and the thinking they'd used to get to those answers. Because of these well-established patterns, all their cognitive energy would be focused on figuring out my big question: How do mental images help when taking a standardized math test?

"You all get to be researchers *and* mathematicians today. The first thing I want to do is think aloud with one of the test samples I brought with me. Your job will be to write down everything you see me do or hear me say as I work through the problem. We'll chart what you notice, and then you'll have a chance to do the same sort of work with a different math problem."

I turned on the overhead and began working through the problem of drawing a five-sided shape. "Hmm, the directions say that I need to draw a figure, a closed shape, with five sides. One of the sides has to be three inches long. And I need to label that side."

As I continued to talk my way through the problem, Sarah's students jotted down what they saw and heard.

"What did you notice?" I asked.

Mackenzie started. "The first thing you did was read the directions. You even said that the words *draw* and *figure* meant that you'd need a picture."

"Yeah, then you used your fingers to estimate how long three inches would be. You were picturing how long an inch was," Sam said.

"No, first you used your background knowledge about how test makers normally put a test together. You knew that your answer had to fit in the empty box," Sarah H. corrected.

"You thought about how big the shape should be in your head," Madi said.

"And then when you started to draw it, you said 'the way it needed to be.' It was like you figured out what the shape was and made sure it matched with the question," Blake added.

"And when you were finished, you said, 'That's as perfect as I can make it . . . Is that what the people want it to look like?' So you were thinking about the picture the test makers had in their head as you worked," Jack finished.

I jotted everything they mentioned in the white space surrounding the test question. "You all really noticed a lot! Now it's your turn. I have six or seven different test items that you can choose from. Remember, your job is not only to take the test, but to keep track of the ways you're creating mental images. Write down any of your thinking in the margins and be ready to share when we come back together."

Students headed off, and Sarah and I let them settle into a busy hum. Because they were so used to collaborating with one another, a number of students clumped together, sharing their math work and their math thinking.

Shyla and Jordan were busy constructing the animal graph they needed to answer number eleven (see Figure 5.8). As they developed similar graphs, their conversation gave me insight into their thinking.

Figure 5.8

Mathematics

11   Tameka collected the following information about different kinds of pets her classmates own.

What kind of pet do you own?

Animal	Tally	Number
Cats	ʜʜ ʜʜ llll	14
Dogs	ʜʜ ʜʜ ʜʜ ll	17
Birds	ʜʜ l	6
Other	llll	4

Mathematics

11   (continued)

Construct a bar graph using the data Tameka collected. Be sure to include:

- an informative title
- a scale
- all the categories of animals
- a label for the scale
- a label for the categories.

"See how the bar has to go way up here if we have each box stand for one animal?" Jordan said. (She pointed to the top of the page as she talked). "That would work if we were just doing this problem for Ms. Grubb because the picture would match the numbers."

"But this is a test," Shyla added. "They're only going to grade what's in the space, so we have to make it fit." She began to write "You're going to need more space" beside her graph.

"Tell me more about what you've figured out about this problem," I interrupted.

"Because this is a test, I'd need to renumber the lines to fit seventeen squares, maybe like three, six, nine, twelve, so I wouldn't go over the lines," Jordan explained. As I jotted this smart thinking on her paper, she added, "That way my picture matches the test maker's picture."

Sitting across the table from the girls, Diego shared, "I first wrote the numbers in lightly because I thought it would go too high. It has to fit seventeen. So then I numbered it by twos and since it fit, I traced over it in pen." Sarah quickly transcribed Diego's words so he'd be able to share them with the group at the end of the workshop.

I moved on to Sam. He was busy working on the spinner problem (see Figure 5.9).

"There are three yellows and only two reds," he said. "There are more yellows. I can actually picture myself spinning it [the wheel], and I'm thinking that if I'm yellow, I have a better chance. Sometimes in these games the top or the bottom might have a better chance if the parts aren't all the same size. I have to check to see if they're all the same size."

I walked away as Sam wrote all this thinking in the margins of the test. I overheard Sarah H. and Mackenzie coming to the shared conclusion that "you shouldn't go off the lines because they [the test makers] might mark it wrong." They knew that their answer had to fit into the space given—an important image constraint of tests. And I listened in on Riley as he shared his thinking with his table: "I noticed that Charlie thought three was three . . .

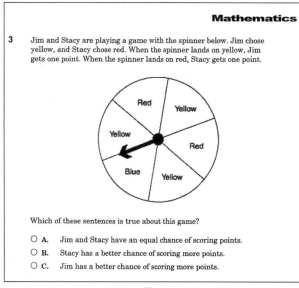

Mathematics

3   Jim and Stacy are playing a game with the spinner below. Jim chose yellow, and Stacy chose red. When the spinner lands on yellow, Jim gets one point. When the spinner lands on red, Stacy gets one point.

Which of these sentences is true about this game?

○ **A.**   Jim and Stacy have an equal chance of scoring points.
○ **B.**   Stacy has a better chance of scoring more points.
○ **C.**   Jim has a better chance of scoring more points.

Figure 5.9

Figure 5.10

Mathematics

7   Charlie says that both straws below are the same length because each one is 3 paper clips long.

Explain the mistakes in Charlie's thinking. Use words, numbers, or pictures.

16

three big ones [paper clips] were the same as three small ones. If he used small ones on the longer straw, he'd need more. I tried to picture the three big ones on the small straw and they wouldn't fit." (See Figure 5.10.)

After thirty minutes of math thinking, we gathered back on the carpet to list our conclusions. We discovered that mathematicians created mental images to help them make sense of their work (see Figure 5.11).

"Of these smart conclusions, are there any that seem to apply just to tests?" I asked.

Sarah H. summed it up for us. "Probably only the last one. It's like our writing. Can we go off the lines with our writing? Yeah, if it's just in our notebooks. But if it's on a test, they'll mark it wrong. I guess it's just like that on math tests."

POSSIBILITIES: Craft Lessons for Creating Mental Images

How can our images help us track the location of specific details referred to in a question?

Practice keeping an ongoing mental snapshot or test image to quickly refer to specific sections while answering questions. (E.g., the character was described in the second paragraph; the temperature column was the last column on the graph.)

What should our work look like when it's finished?

Outline the various ways tests specify how complete answers should look, and what content complete answers should contain. (E.g., "Since the test gives me five lines to write my answer, I know they're looking for more than a word or two. I'll need to include specific details to get a good score." "The answer box is pretty small. I'll probably just need to write a number without any explanation.")

Since the evaluator will never meet us, how can we provide a true picture of who we are as readers, writers, and so on?

Explore ways students can create a strong, positive portrait of themselves for the test evaluator. (E.g., "I want to be very precise with both the words and numbers I include in my answers." "Have I added enough detail so that the evaluator will know who I am as a learner?")

What happens when our mental images distract us from completing a test item?

Distinguish relevant from irrelevant images. (E.g., "I know it doesn't ask me about the birds, but I can't help but imagine the different kinds of birds who might live in one of these birdhouses. But that's not going to help me answer the questions about building a birdhouse from the

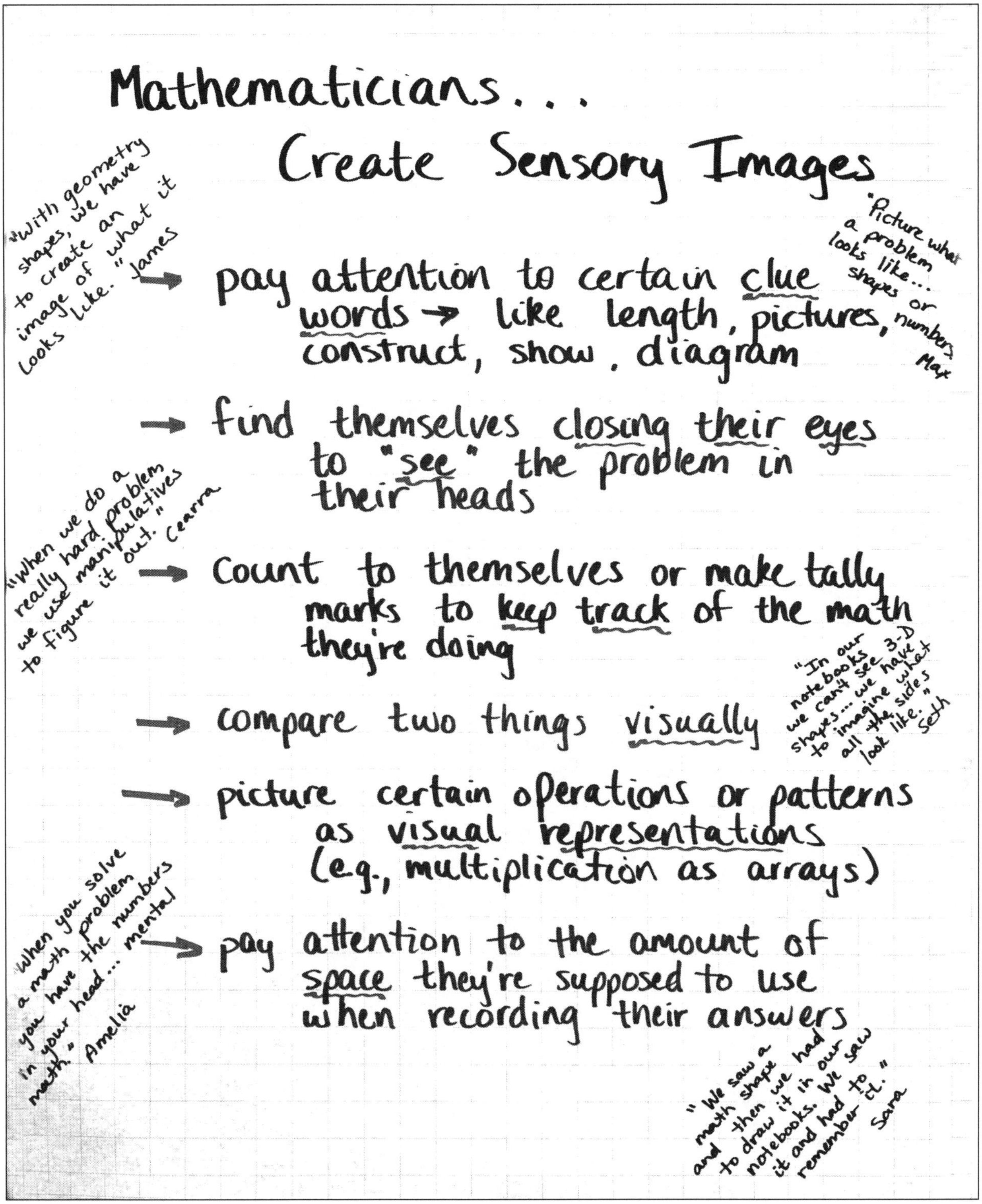

Mathematicians...
Create Sensory Images

"With geometry shapes, we have to create an image of what it looks like." James

"Picture what a problem looks like... shapes or numbers Max

→ **pay attention to certain <u>clue</u> <u>words</u>** → like length, pictures, construct, show, diagram

→ **find themselves <u>closing their eyes</u> to "see" the problem in their heads**

"When we do a really hard problem we use manipulatives to figure it out." Cearra

→ **Count to themselves or make tally marks to <u>keep track</u> of the math they're doing**

"In our notebooks we can't see 3-D shapes... we have to imagine what all the sides look like." Seth

→ **compare two things <u>visually</u>**

→ **picture certain operations or patterns as <u>visual representations</u> (e.g., multiplication as arrays)**

"When you solve a math problem you have the numbers in your head... mental math." Amelia

→ **pay attention to the amount of <u>space</u> they're supposed to use when recording their answers**

" We saw a math shape we had and then we had to draw it in our notebooks. We saw it and had to remember it." Sara

Figure 5.11

directions they give me." "I can picture all kinds of arrays . . . 8 x 4, 6 x 6, 10 x 5, but I probably should concentrate on picturing just one that is 9 x 12.")

What images would we naturally create to help us understand if this wasn't meant specifically for a test?
Describe sensory details that enhance students' ongoing understanding. (E.g., "I can see the four kids dividing the pieces of candy." "I can sense that in this poem, the dog is very ill.")

Chapter 6
TEST TAKERS Draw Inferences

As we work to acquire new knowledge, the inferences we make give us additional ideas to ground and deepen our learning. These inferences help us make discoveries about our world, understand other people's intentions or actions, and make sense of unfamiliar situations.

Recently, Missy and her two-year-old daughter, Rachel, looked out the window to see the neighbor boy, Jacob, standing on his patio holding his BB gun, head slumped, eyes on the ground. Missy's husband, Steve, was talking to him. Rachel said, "Mom, Jacob is sad." What she didn't know at the time was that Jacob's BBs, intended for his fence, were ricocheting off the fence and onto their porch. Rachel inferred how Jacob was feeling by looking at his body language and using her schema for how someone looks when they aren't terribly happy. Rachel understood the situation, and Jacob's feelings, not because it was explained to her, but because she could use clues to come to her own inferred understanding.

As is the case in all classrooms, primary-grade teachers observe their students inferring every day. Young writers' knowledge of spelling develops as they infer about the ways the sounds of our language match various letters and letter patterns. When working to spell the "long *a*," /ā/, sound in the word *cake*, a first grader relies on her background knowledge to recall possible spelling options. A "long *a*" sound can be spelled "*a* consonant *e*" (like in the word *place*), just *a* (like in the name *April*), or *ay* (like in the word *stay*). Her inferred approximations narrow the range of possibilities from which she can choose.

Test takers face many situations requiring them to infer. Sometimes they have to guess about the intent behind a certain question or draw a conclusion about an expected response. Just like Rachel, test takers rely on their background knowledge about test questions and formats to determine what they're supposed to do and how they're supposed to show what they know.

To do this, test takers . . .

- figure out a test item's unwritten, or under-written, purpose. ("They want me to look for commonalities between these two graphs. This question must be checking to see if I can 'read between the lines' to understand similarities between two data sources." "They're asking me for only the facts. This isn't a place where they want my thinking that supports my answer.")

- anticipate a test question's expectations. ("It looks like I'll need to subtract first and then divide. They want to know if I can do two-step math problems.")

- determine the meaning of individual words or phrases. ("The phrase *hard facts* must mean choice A: 'the difficult realities in life,' because the author has described all the challenges the main character has had to endure. In that context, A must be the answer.")

- uncover the purpose or author motive for individual test passages. ("I'm thinking this piece was written to tell a reader that people can choose to be happy. That's a lot like number two: 'the author is trying to convince the reader that happiness is a choice.' I'll pick that for my answer.")

- decipher the genre-specific test language that signals certain action. ("The question says, 'Which answer is the best choice?' I bet there'll be several possible answers and I'll need to pick the best one." "When the test says, 'According to the story, . . .' I know I'll need to use specific words from the story to choose the correct answer." "When the question says, 'What do you think will happen next?' they must be asking me to include some of my opinion in my written response.")

Student Examples—Naming What They Notice About Tests and Drawing Inferences

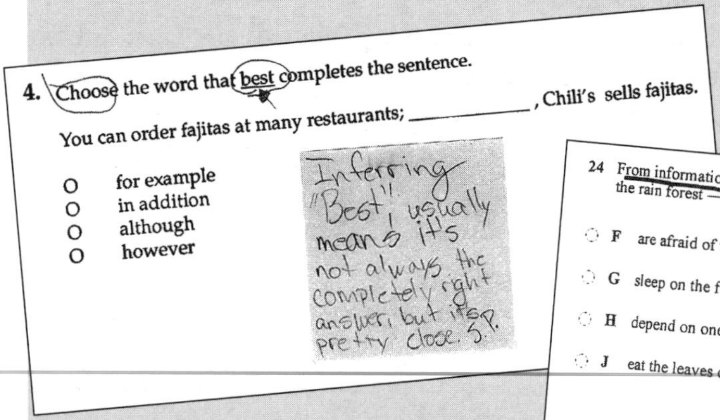

4. Choose the word that *best* completes the sentence.

You can order fajitas at many restaurants; _____, Chili's sells fajitas.

O   for example
O   in addition
O   although
O   however

Inferring
"Best" usually
means it's
not always the
completely right
answer, but it's
pretty close. :)

Figure 6.1. Using what she knows about test vocabulary, Samantha infers that *best* really means "pretty close."

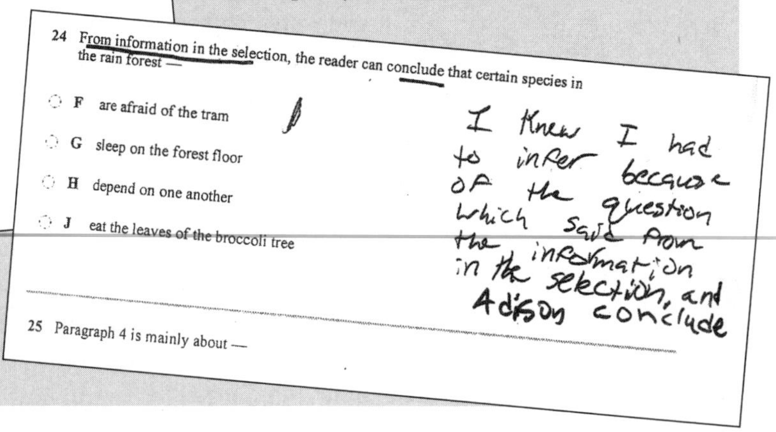

24   From information in the selection, the reader can conclude that certain species in the rain forest —

O   F   are afraid of the tram
O   G   sleep on the forest floor
O   H   depend on one another
O   J   eat the leaves of the broccoli tree

I knew I had
to infer because
of the question
which said from
the information
in the selection, and
Adison conclude

25   Paragraph 4 is mainly about —

Figure 6.2. Here, Adison, a fourth grader, uses the structure of the test question to cue his inference.

Student Examples—Naming What They Notice About Tests and Drawing Inferences

Figure 6.3. Ellary highlights the word *probably* and explains how that word lets her know she needs to infer.

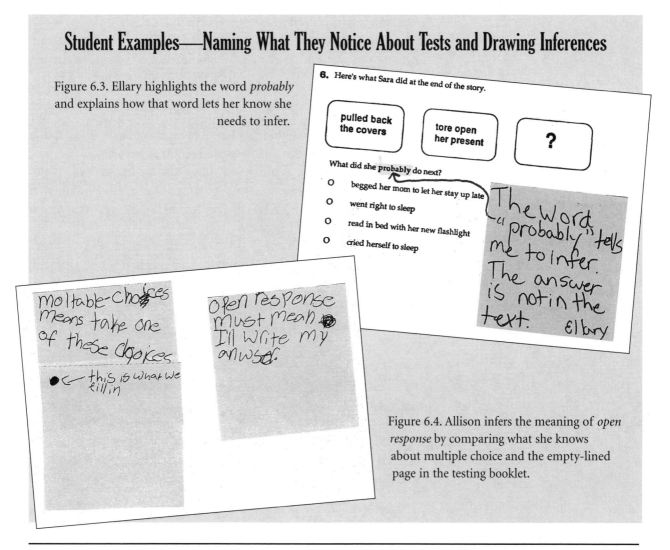

Figure 6.4. Allison infers the meaning of *open response* by comparing what she knows about multiple choice and the empty-lined page in the testing booklet.

STORIES FROM THE CLASSROOM

Extending Fourth Graders' Study of Inferring

By Lori L. Conrad

"Inferring is when you have to put your own words into the story," Patrick shared.

"Yeah, because it's the thinking and ideas the author doesn't tell you," Kamren added.

"You have to use your background knowledge, your schema," Maureen chimed in.

"It's like making a smart guess, an estimate. But it isn't just predicting. It can go deeper than that," Molly concluded.

As I recorded all this thinking on a new classroom chart, it was clear that Angel's students had already done a lot of work defining for themselves just what inferring was and how making an inference helped someone, anyone, understand what they were doing—reading, writing, solving math problems, researching, living.

"It's like when I go home and my mom has that face . . . I know I'm in trouble! She doesn't even have to say a word. Her look tells me all I need to know," Tucker said, and all his classmates nodded in agreement.

"Making an inference is figuring out ideas and words that aren't just sitting on the surface . . . You have to peel back meaning by adding your schema to what's on the page," I said as I added the following visual to our chart (see the top portion of Figure 6.5).

"It's like an addition problem," I said, "one a thinker creates in his head as he's trying to make sense of a situation—make sense beyond what's on the surface. When you're making an inference, what would your in-your-head voice be saying to you?" The class named four different examples: "I think . . .," "I predict . . .," "I guess that . . .," and "I infer . . ." I added these to the chart.

Figure 6.5

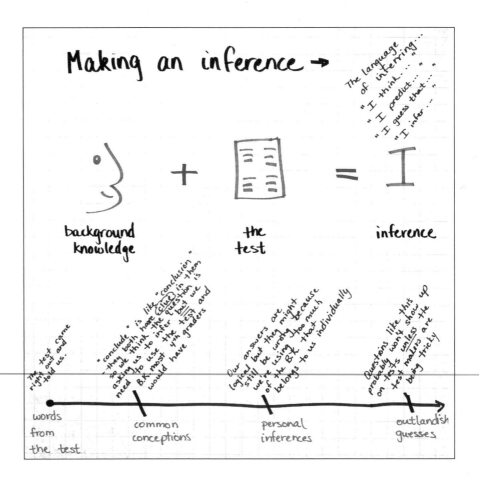

"From what you've already learned about making inferences, you've figured out that inferring helps us understand complex writing and implied meanings. So, how does being able to make an inference help you when you're taking a test? Turn to a neighbor and talk for a couple of minutes." As the students talked with the person sitting next to them, I added the following "picture" to our chart:

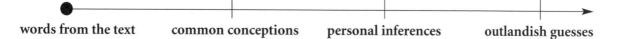

words from the text   **common conceptions**   **personal inferences**   **outlandish guesses**

"When we read the newspaper or a story, the inferences we make might be pretty similar to just about any other reader's," I said. "We're drawing those inferences from some shared background knowledge the author assumes anyone reading his article or story would have. Sometimes, however, our inferences might be different from other readers'. They're different because we're using more of our own unique schema to come to those conclusions. Even if they're different, these inferences can still help us make sense. Let's call those 'personal inferences.'

"But we also know our inferences can be distracting if they're so far away from the text they no longer help us make meaning. I'm going to label these 'outlandish guesses' because they're silly and really mean we're not understanding what we're reading.

"Remember when we talked about using our schema and test taking? Remember how we decided that test makers have to create an even or level playing field if a whole bunch of fourth graders have to take the same test? The test makers can't write a test that relies on the different background knowledge each of you brings with you to school. We also figured out that the test makers have to write a test that includes enough information so you can get the right answers either from the words on the test or from what I'm going to call a 'test inference'—an inference that's close enough to the test that different readers can come to the same conclusions even if they don't share the same personal background knowledge.

"I've got another test sample for you guys to try. This time, it's one taken by kids in Texas. It's a nonfiction piece about visiting the rain forest. As you read through it, pay attention to when you have to infer, both to understand the story and to answer the questions. Keep track of your thinking in the margins and be ready to share new insights in about twenty-five minutes."

Students grabbed the released passage and headed back to their seats. After a few minutes, Angel and I conferred with a few students who had begun answering the questions.

When I looked over Tanner's shoulder, he shared: "I'm on number twenty-three, the one with the web [see Figure 6.6]. I looked at the first circle that was already filled in, the one that says 'open on the sides,' and I had to

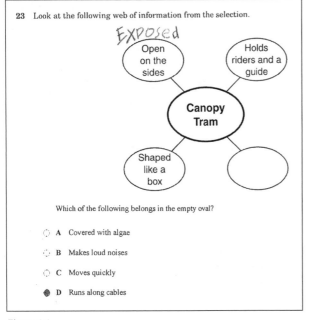

23   Look at the following web of information from the selection.

Which of the following belongs in the empty oval?

○ A   Covered with algae

○ B   Makes loud noises

○ C   Moves quickly

● D   Runs along cables

Figure 6.6

guess that meant the same thing as the sentence 'The sides of the tram are exposed so that people can see, smell, and hear everything.' The word *exposed* means the same as open. So when the test makers wrote the web, they didn't use the exact words from the story, just some of them or some that were close. So the answer to this question is 'runs along cables.' That's close to what the story said."

We headed over to see what Kamren was busy doing. He was erasing his answer to number twenty-eight. Along the side, he'd written, "*I used B.K. [background knowledge] more then [than] test info*" (see Figure 6.7).

"At first I thought they'd go to bed early because they were tired," he said. "The trip was long and it took all day. I know what that's like. My family takes those kinds of trips all the time. But then I was thinking that maybe not all fourth graders would know that. So I went back into the story and found the part that said, 'We went to bed early to prepare for the adventure ahead of us.' That sounded a lot like choice F—'They want to be well rested for the tour the next morning.'"

"So, your first answer made sense to you, but didn't make sense for the test?" I asked.

"I guess my inference was too far from the words in the test," Kamren admitted.

Angel and I conferred with a few more students and discovered the many ways they were inferring (see Figure 6.8).

As we gathered back in the whole-group area to share what we'd figured out, we added a few new ideas to the ray on our chart (see the bottom of Figure 6.5).

Angel and I then made notes about lessons she'd plan for the next few days:

- What sorts of test words "cue" a reader to know she's supposed to infer?
- How do we monitor our natural instinct to use too much of our schema, knowing the difference between a potentially logical answer and the right answer?
- How do test takers make inferences to understand the texts included in the tests as well as the questions on the tests?
- How can we recognize possible answers that make sense in a general way, but aren't directly linked to the test (e.g., intentionally misleading options)?

Figure 6.7

28 Why do Enrique and his parents go to bed early after arriving at the lodge?

● F   They want to be well rested for the tour the next morning.

○ G   The sound of the birds of the rain forest puts them to sleep.

○ H   They are tired after the long airplane trip from Dallas.

○ J   The tour guide tells them that the tram ride the next day will be difficult.

I used Bokg more then test info

Figure 6.8. In these samples, fourth graders Carter, Carsyn, Molly, Jacob, and Kilian share the ways they infer to find the correct response on multiple-choice questions.

24 From information in the selection, the reader can conclude that certain species in the rain forest —

○ F   are afraid of the tram

○ G   sleep on the forest floor

● H   depend on one another

○ J   eat the leaves of the broccoli tree

Carter

I pnFrd en exdfl is haw theAlgl giv the stuth camig

(I inferred an example is how the algae gives the sloth camouflage)

22 From information in the selection, the reader can tell that the rain forest in Costa Rica is —

○ F   a little-known vacation spot

○ G   full of loud noises

● H   home to some unusual animals

○ J   dangerous for humans

Carsyn

you can infer because of the animals they list

21 Why does Enrique write that this trip is the best thing that ever happened to him?

○ A   He has dreamed of riding through the rain forest on a canopy tram.

○ B   He had to work hard to write an essay about the rain forest.

○ C   He has always wanted to take a trip with his parents.

● D   He has been interested in rain forests since he was a small child.

Molly

words inthis question it come right out and teys you he has wanted to go to the rainforests sinse hewas five

Figure 6.8. *continued*

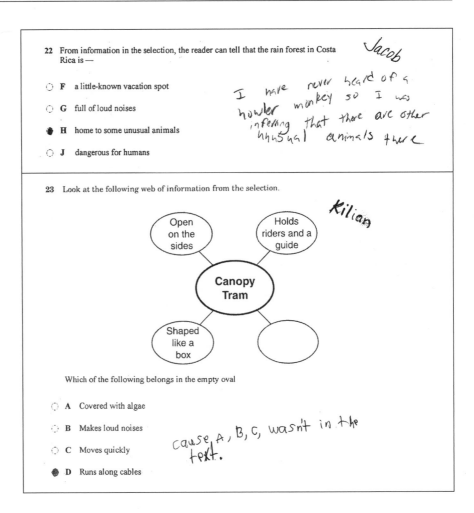

22 From information in the selection, the reader can tell that the rain forest in Costa Rica is —

Jacob

○ F a little-known vacation spot

○ G full of loud noises

● H home to some unusual animals

○ J dangerous for humans

I have never heard of a howler monkey so I was inferring that there are other unusual animals there

23 Look at the following web of information from the selection.

Kilian

Open on the sides

Holds riders and a guide

Canopy Tram

Shaped like a box

Which of the following belongs in the empty oval

○ A Covered with algae

○ B Makes loud noises

○ C Moves quickly

● D Runs along cables

cause, A, B, C, wasn't in the text.

Inferring with Middle School Scientists

By Missy Matthews

Andy's sixth graders had spent the past four weeks exploring the inferences scientists make as they "do" science. As part of this exploration, students coded expository articles, marking places where they knew they were inferring and the ways those inferences helped them understand. They also noted their thinking while conducting experiments, describing how inferences helped them anticipate and understand their work. Andy and his students talked about the word *hypothesis* and how that term signals the ways scientists infer a possible outcome or outcomes of an experiment or scientific inquiry.

Andy integrated these discussions about inferring with a district-mandated curricular unit on the states of matter. He created focus for this unit by asking two essential questions:

- How does matter change states?
- How can we explain changes in the natural world using what we know about states of matter?

Because thinking strategies had become a schoolwide instructional focus, these students weren't just thinking about inferences as scientists. When they went to their math class, they talked about the kinds of inferences mathematicians make to understand problems. When they were in social studies, the conversations centered on the kinds of inferences historians make when working to understand ancient cultures. And when they read and wrote in their language arts class, their teacher asked them to consider how inferring helped them comprehend and compose.

On this day, I joined the class to explore how the students might extend their thinking beyond their daily work into their work as test takers. Our conversation began with a definition of *inferring*. Matt said that to make an inference, "You make a guess."

Miranda shared that an inference isn't any old guess. "When we infer, our thinking has to be based on facts or evidence from the text."

Dixon chimed in, "To make an inference, you use the text and your background knowledge." We translated this into a mathematical equation: BK + Text = Inference. Then he added that another way we infer is "to take numbers and facts from a problem and estimate an answer."

Zach shared that visualizing helps him infer because he can see the problem in his head, and Matt added that when he's able to determine importance, he's making an inference, also.

Because this was the first time students had talked about thinking as test takers, I decided to start by modeling. I chose to think aloud and ask students to report out what they saw and heard.

With a transparency of a released item on the overhead, I shared my thinking (see Figure 6.9). "As I look at this first page, I see the bold directions here at the top. I'm going to start there, because it will help me set a purpose for the kind of work I'll do. In the directions, it says 'choose the BEST answer.' I'm inferring that there may be several answers I could reason through, but I'll need to pick the one answer that makes the most sense.

"These directions look a lot like the kind of directions you see on a test like CSAP. I bet this will

Figure 6.9

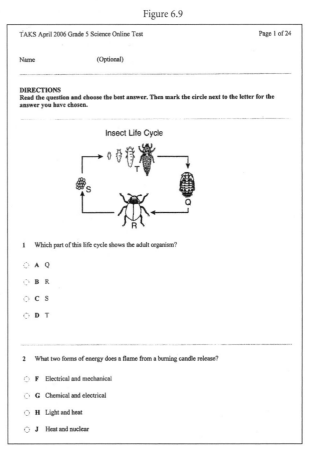

be a multiple-choice test where I'll read a question and then have to sift and sort through the answers to decide which one to choose. I know I often find tricky answers, so I'll have to be aware of places where the test maker is really trying to figure out if I know which answer is best.

"I realize that when I take a test, I scan the page and the questions to make inferences about the kind of work I'll be doing. For instance, there's this diagram with two questions that follow. I'm inferring that the questions following the diagram will ask about the diagram, almost like the test is set up in sections. Oh, wait, the second question is about energy, so I think my inference is wrong. Only question number one will be about the diagram.

"There are letters beside each stage of the life cycle on the diagram. I'm inferring that I'll use the letters to choose a label for each stage.

"In question number one, it asks me to label the adult organism. It will help me if I label all of the parts to make sure I know which one is the adult. So, here are the eggs, the larvae, and the pupa, and this must be the adult. I'll choose letter R.

"As I think about question two, 'What two forms of energy does a flame from a burning candle release?' I don't know the answer right away. I'm going to have to look through the choices to see if I can make a reasonable guess. That's going to be an inference.

"I don't think it could be choice F, 'electrical and mechanical,' because a candle flame isn't electrical or mechanical. I also don't think it could be choice G, 'chemical and electrical,' because there's nothing electrical about a candle flame. So that rules out options F and G. H makes sense to me because a candle is a chemical reaction using light and heat. J says 'heat and nuclear.' I'm pretty sure it's not nuclear, since I light candles in my house all the time. So, by inferring what could and could not be possible, I'm narrowing my options. I'm going with H."

With an intentional pause, I looked back to the students and asked, "What did you see me doing?"

Justin started off. "When you said it's like a CSAP test, you related it to something you already know about to create a plan."

"You wrote down what you were thinking, and then you chose the best answers. The only problem with this is that we can't write on our CSAPs," Hayden added.

"After you decided what was most important in a question, like that the question asked about the adult organism, then you could figure out what it couldn't be," shared Jessica.

Sarah said, "You were inferring about how the test was set up."

Cierra added, "You first made inferences about parts of the answers that you could eliminate, and then you could choose from what was left."

After charting the students' responses, I invited students to give this a try in pairs or trios. "Now I want you to try this yourselves. Notice the inferences you make as you work through this test and jot them down so you can share your thinking with the rest of the class when we gather back together to reflect."

Students found desks and floor space, and gathered into small clusters. I moved throughout the classroom, observing and noting their conversations. I looked and listened for any thinking that might benefit the whole group.

After twenty-five minutes, we gathered back together at the front of the room. I had overheads of each page from the test on which to record student thinking. The first question was a problem about the rate of freezing water in two different freezers.

Dixon shared that his group had narrowed it down to two choices and then determined that two words were most important in the answers. "It was either *temperature* or *time*, but we weren't sure which was correct. We went with *temperature*, answer A."

"So, your group inferred that one of two words signaled the correct choice? And then you were able to eliminate two of the four answers, giving you a fifty-fifty chance at being right?" Dixon nodded.

"We inferred how fast it would freeze," Ruben said. I recorded Ruben's response on the overhead and decided this thinking would be a great teaching point for another day, because the way his group was thinking about the problem wouldn't get them to the right answer. This would be an important conversation about how tests are set up. Test makers often include answers that anticipate incorrect inferences about the problem. This group's work would be a natural link to understanding this all-too-typical testing trap.

The heart of our reflection came as we talked about the third question. To answer this question, students had to compare and analyze information from two different charts. Sarah shared that she thought the answer was C, because she knew black bears lived in the mountains. Brian raised his hand and said that he agreed with Sarah's answer, but for a different reason. "If you look at the chart called 'Black Bear Needs,' it has fruit as a food they eat, and only one of the habitats in the chart called 'Characteristics of Four Habitats' has any fruits."

When I looked at Sarah's paper, she had crossed out the bottom chart because she thought it was extraneous information, whereas Brian had made the case that he needed both charts to actually confirm an answer. This led to a great discussion about how relying on our background knowledge outside of the testing situation isn't always the safest strategy. Brian proved to us that test makers are looking for something specific. As test takers, it's our job to figure out those specifics.

Our work concluded by creating the anchor chart shown in Figure 6.10.

Figure 6.10

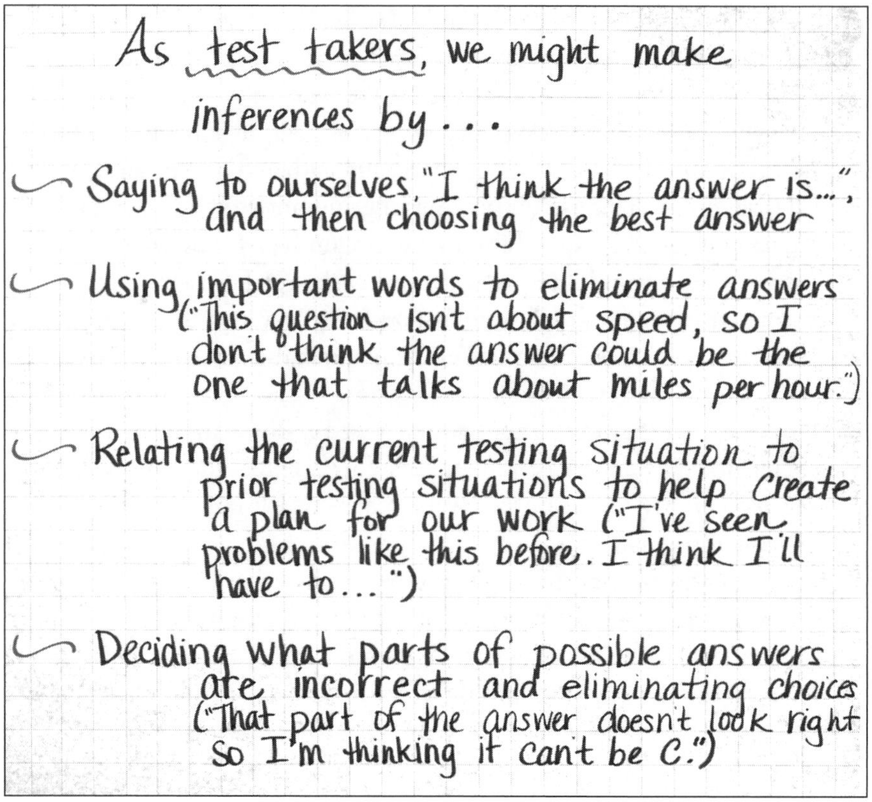

> As **test takers**, we might make inferences by . . .
>
> ↪ Saying to ourselves, "I think the answer is...", and then choosing the best answer
>
> ↪ Using important words to eliminate answers ("This question isn't about speed, so I don't think the answer could be the one that talks about miles per hour.")
>
> ↪ Relating the current testing situation to prior testing situations to help create a plan for our work ("I've seen problems like this before. I think I'll have to... ")
>
> ↪ Deciding what parts of possible answers are incorrect and eliminating choices ("That part of the answer doesn't look right so I'm thinking it can't be C.")

POSSIBILITIES: Craft Lessons for Drawing Inferences

What clues can we use that will immediately help us with a test item?
Predict test genre and content based on surface clues and text features. (E.g., "I'll bet this is about number patterns because it looks just like an in-and-out box." "This is probably nonfiction because it has headings and captions.")

When is it best to be explicit with our answers rather than expect that someone will infer what we mean?
Eliminate vagueness from the test evaluator's mind. (E.g., "I can't explain what I mean in person, so I better add details to my answer." "This is a paragraph about my dog, but it might not be clear to anyone who doesn't know Skipper. I better name what I'm doing for my reader.")

What words do test makers use that signal we're supposed to be inferring?
Identify specific question words that tell a test taker to infer. (E.g., "This says 'about how many,' so I know I can estimate to find an answer." "The

question asks, 'What will most likely occur next?' *Most likely* means I'm supposed to infer. I won't find the exact answer in the test.")

When are our inferences really nothing more than distractions?
Check accuracy, reasonableness, and usefulness of predictions, assumptions, and conclusions in terms of test content. (E.g., "I kept thinking about how boring it would be to have to watch the same plants grow over months and months, and that probably isn't what I should include in my written summary of the experiment." "I'm guessing the character's mom was pretty mad about him stealing the money from her purse, but since there aren't any questions about the mom, that inference won't really help me." "Did I use my schema too much to answer this problem?")

How does inferring work for us in contexts other than standardized tests?
Define the characteristics of inferences in a variety of texts and content. (E.g., "I know this is a poem. It doesn't have very many words, but I know it has layers of meaning. I'll have to 'read between the lines' to really understand what the poet is saying." "I know this math page is about division, so I'll need to remember that I can use multiplication to check my answer.")

Chapter 7
TEST TAKERS Synthesize New Learning and Ideas

Many believe synthesis is one of the "higher-level thinking skills" that belongs in classes for gifted students. They think it's too "conceptually challenging" for those students who haven't reached the formal operational stage of cognition.

In reality, synthesis is the *very thing* that allows any of us to learn from our mistakes, grow in our understandings, develop new insights, or change our opinions. Without the capacity to synthesize, our thinking gets stuck.

In an age-old rite of passage, Lori's son, Nathanael, just earned his driver's license. For an entire year, Nathanael's knowledge of driving a car evolved. At first, his understanding was limited to what he'd observed from the backseat and what he'd read in *Car and Driver*. After receiving his permit, the question "Now what do I think about driving?" echoed in his head. He gathered input from his dad, his mom, a driving instructor, driving manuals, and videos such as *Blood on the Highway*.

At the end of his twelve-month apprenticeship, Nathanael had to synthesize it all. His new understandings about driving included threads of his initial views, but it was more than a simple accumulation of facts. As his nervous parents watched him leave on his first solo drive, Nathanael put into practice an enriched, personally meaningful understanding of the demands and dangers of driving a car.

Historians spend an entire lifetime studying a time period, a culture, or a region of the world, synthesizing new information into their established understandings and beliefs. For example, those who've long studied the plight of concentration-camp victims and survivors add, change, revise, and extend their knowledge. With each victim interview, discovery of evidence, or review of another expert's writing, historians synthesize new thinking into their current knowledge.

Test takers also synthesize information. They're able to play the game of test taking. Their understanding of the unique demands and the importance of demonstrating what they know during testing situations evolves and becomes more sophisticated over time.

A test taker must . . .

· navigate unfamiliar testing situations. ("I've never taken this test before, but I know from the directions there will be three writing sessions. It could either be three separate sessions—one focused on isolated editing and grammar tasks, one focused on drafting short responses, and one focused on composing one longer piece—or each session could be a mix of all the things a writer needs to know how to do.")

· approach testing situations with a plan. ("I notice this section of the test has two different passages to read and three different sets of questions. The final set of questions asks me to compare the two passages. I'm going to read both passages knowing I'll need to compare them at the end.")

· formulate answers flexibly to fit the testing situation. ("When I take the district writing test, the evaluators don't ask to see any planning. But when I take the state test, they give me a page for my planning. For that test, I'll need to make sure the plan makes good sense to the evaluators.")

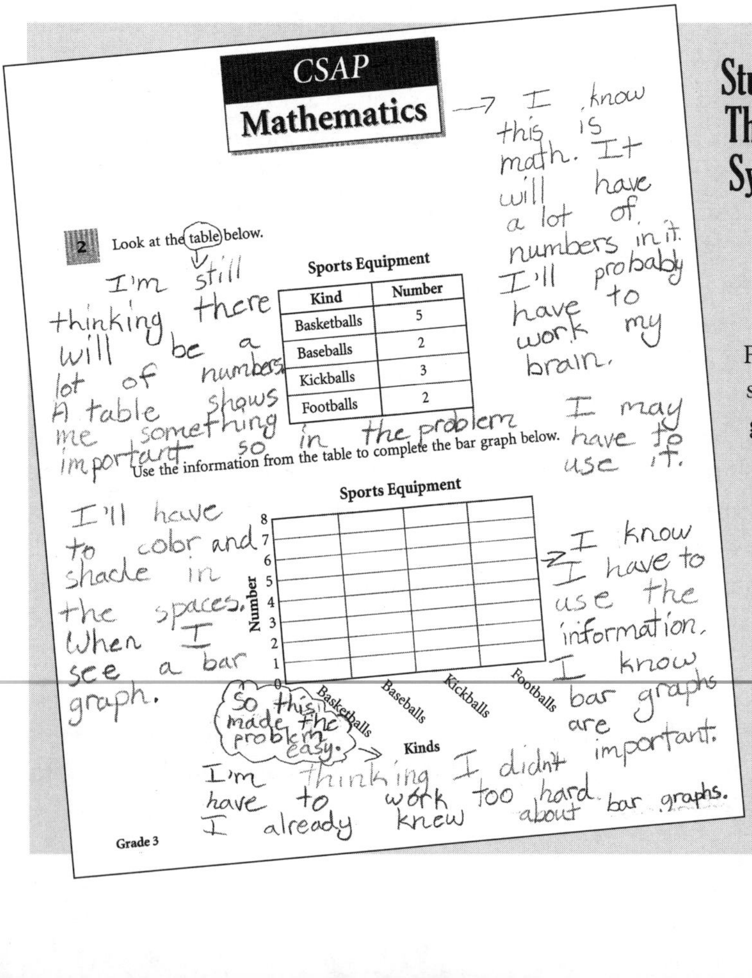

Student Examples—Naming What They Notice About Tests and Synthesizing

Figure 7.1. As a third grader, Lauryn uses what she knows about bar graphs to develop a generalization. Synthesizing allows her to form a personal opinion about this test problem's complexity.

Student Examples—Naming What They Notice About Tests and Synthesizing

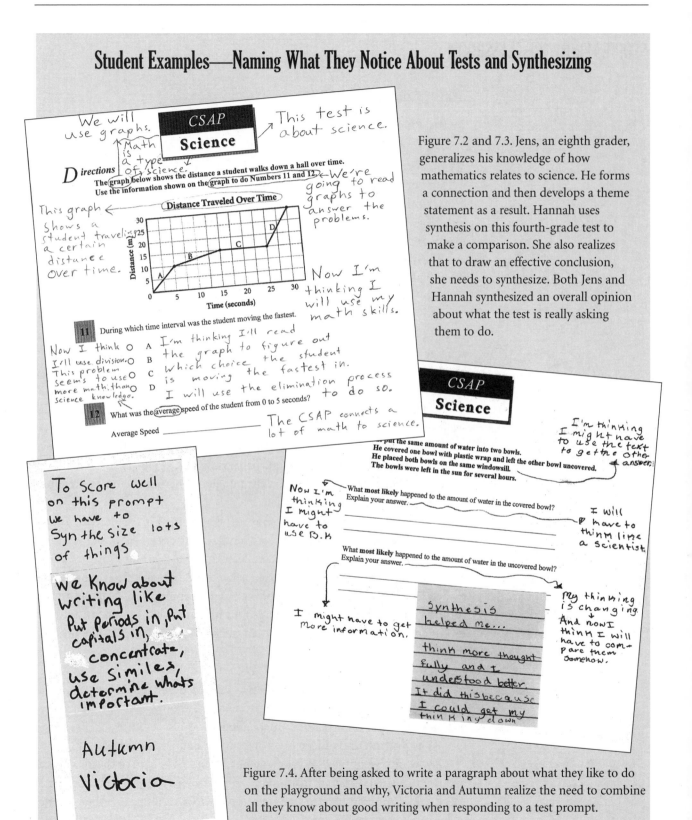

We will use graphs.

Math is a type of science.

This test is about science.

CSAP
Science

Directions
The graph below shows the distance a student walks down a hall over time. Use the information shown on the graph to do Numbers 11 and 12.

We're going to read graphs to answer the problems.

This graph shows a student traveling a certain distance over time.

Distance Traveled Over Time

Now I'm thinking I will use my math skills.

11 During which time interval was the student moving the fastest.

Now I think I'll use division. This problem seems to use more math than science knowledge.

O A
O B
O C
O D

I'm thinking I'll read the graph to figure out which choice the student is moving the fastest in. I will use the elimination process to do so.

12 What was the average speed of the student from 0 to 5 seconds?

Average Speed _____

The CSAP connects a lot of math to science.

Figure 7.2 and 7.3. Jens, an eighth grader, generalizes his knowledge of how mathematics relates to science. He forms a connection and then develops a theme statement as a result. Hannah uses synthesis on this fourth-grade test to make a comparison. She also realizes that to draw an effective conclusion, she needs to synthesize. Both Jens and Hannah synthesized an overall opinion about what the test is really asking them to do.

CSAP
Science

...put the same amount of water into two bowls. He covered one bowl with plastic wrap and left the other bowl uncovered. He placed both bowls on the same windowsill. The bowls were left in the sun for several hours.

I'm thinking I might have to use the text to get the other answer.

Now I'm thinking I might have to use B.K

What most likely happened to the amount of water in the covered bowl? Explain your answer. _____

I will have to think like a scientist.

What most likely happened to the amount of water in the uncovered bowl? Explain your answer. _____

I might have to get more information.

Synthesis helped me... think more thoughtfully and t understood better. It did this because I could get my thinking down

My thinking is changing. And now I think I will have to compare them somehow.

To Score well on this prompt We have to Synthe size lots of things

We Know about writing like Put Periods in, Put capitals in, concentrate, use Similes, determine whats important.

Autumn

Victoria

Figure 7.4. After being asked to write a paragraph about what they like to do on the playground and why, Victoria and Autumn realize the need to combine all they know about good writing when responding to a test prompt.

STORIES FROM THE CLASSROOM

Synthesizing as Test Takers

By Patrick A. Allen

My third graders and I had been involved in a study of synthesis for about a week when Chauncey said, "It's like a wall. You just keep building, brick by brick, until . . . suddenly you have a wall! It's different. It's changed. Your lingering thoughts keep coming together—they just keep building." Leave it to Chauncey to come up with a fabulous metaphor.

The next day, as I called my students together for our craft lesson, I reminded them to think about Chauncey's metaphor and nudged them to continue thinking of one that might enhance their definitions of synthesis.

"Boys and girls, thanks for joining me so quickly today. I can see that you're all ready to continue our discussion of synthesis. I have to tell you, I can't get Chauncey's great thinking out of my mind. In fact, I was thinking about a new brick we might add to *our* wall. What if we were thinking about synthesis as test takers? I wonder what that might look like." I placed a piece titled "The Deep Sleepers" on the document camera so that the group could see it on the screen.

"Today, we're going to read this article and try to figure out how synthesis might help us understand it. Remember, we'll see these kinds of pieces on CSAP. Take a look and tell me what you're noticing." I gave the students time to glance at the article.

I knew this article would serve as a springboard for further discussion about synthesis. This would be a shared experience. We'd be working through the piece together to build collective understanding.

"Let me tell you why I chose this piece. It did several things for me as a reader: it changed my understanding of hibernation, it helped me to compare and contrast old knowledge and new knowledge, and it captured my interest because it was written in such a unique way. What do you think?"

"It looks like nonfiction," said Chris.

"But it's written like a story," Olivia said. "I don't see any captions, or headings, or any other features that we've talked about."

"It's more like an article," Daniel added.

"Why did you draw those lines on it, Mr. Allen?" Luke asked.

"Wow. You've noticed so many details," I said. "It's a piece that I selected because it looked different from many of the other types of nonfiction text we've read. I thought it would be a good piece to synthesize together. It kind of looks like an article and it kind of looks like a story. I drew the lines to

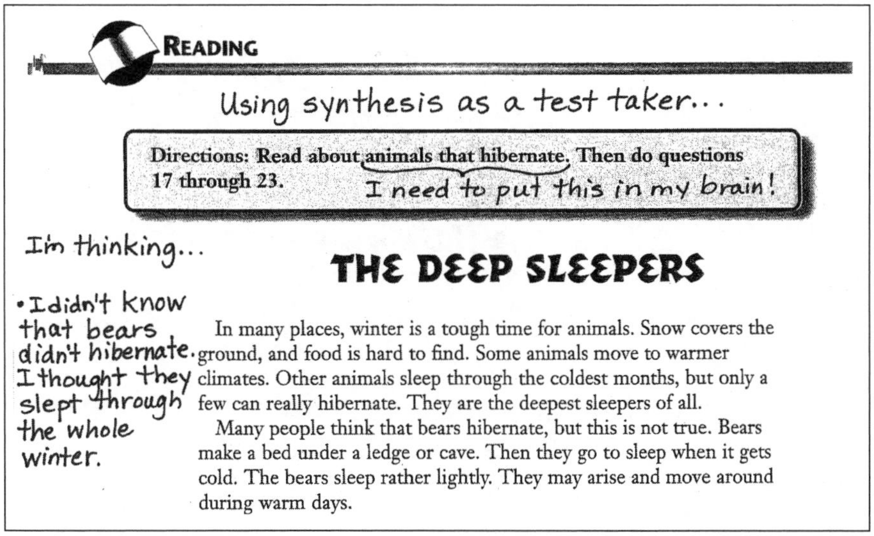

Figure 7.5

> **READING**
>
> *Using synthesis as a test taker...*
>
> **Directions: Read about animals that hibernate. Then do questions 17 through 23.** *I need to put this in my brain!*
>
> *I'm thinking...*
>
> ## THE DEEP SLEEPERS
>
> *• I didn't know that bears didn't hibernate. I thought they slept through the whole winter.*
>
> In many places, winter is a tough time for animals. Snow covers the ground, and food is hard to find. Some animals move to warmer climates. Other animals sleep through the coldest months, but only a few can really hibernate. They are the deepest sleepers of all.
>
> Many people think that bears hibernate, but this is not true. Bears make a bed under a ledge or cave. Then they go to sleep when it gets cold. The bears sleep rather lightly. They may arise and move around during warm days.

divide it into five sections because I thought it might help us if we stopped periodically to talk about our thinking."

I handed out copies of "The Deep Sleepers" to everyone in case they wanted to jot down some of their own thinking as we worked. Having their own copy gave the tactile learners a place to keep track of their thinking, the visual learners something to read, and the auditory learners something to refer to as they listened.

"Let's start with the directions. They say: 'Read about animals that hibernate. Then do questions seventeen through twenty-three.' As I read these directions, I'm thinking we'll probably be reading about more than one animal. We'll need to pay close attention to each section to keep our thinking clear and fresh. Remember, synthesis is about change. We need to keep track of the ways our thinking grows. We want to walk away from this piece with the new understandings necessary to correctly answer the questions at the end. There are seven questions, so we need to read carefully to prove we understood the passage."

"I've learned a lot about how animals hibernate," Jakob interjected.

"I'll bet you have. And that might help you. Today, our job as readers and thinkers will be to read carefully, stop periodically, and jot down our thinking."

As I read the first section, students followed along. "Write down what you're thinking," I encouraged when I stopped and wrote in the margin (see Figure 7.5).

I turned to the class. "As I read this, I was shocked. Usually when you read about hibernation, the first animal you think about is a bear. I've seen so many cartoons showing bears hibernating. This really made me change my thinking. If I have to use the text to answer a question, I better know that

- I'm thinking that it's not true. J.M.
- This piece will tell me about hibernating. N.E.
- Bears do this because they had food. B.F.
- Bears come out on warm days to get food. S.B.
- This piece is nonfiction because it tells facts about bears. A.M.

Figure 7.6

- It's about animals and how they survive when they hibernate. L.R.
- It's going to be about different animals and how they live. T.A.
- They are telling me facts about hibernation...
- Small animals can hibernate too. O.M.
- Now I'm thinking about all hibernators. C.L.

Figure 7.8

Figure 7.7

Now I'm thinking...
- That other animals do hibernate by changing themselves (storing fat, slowing breathing, etc.) But only until spring. Small animals hibernate too!

The real hibernators can put themselves into a mysterious state that is much deeper than sleep. Their bodies may become almost as cold as their surroundings. Their breathing slows down. Their heartbeats get slower. They do not eat or drink. Most hibernators do not even move. They stay that way all winter long until the spring **thaw**.

The ground squirrel is probably the best hibernator of all. Throughout the summer, he stuffs himself with food. By September, he weighs twice as much as he did in May. He will live off this stored body fat for eight months.

the text says, 'Many people think that bears hibernate, but this is not true . . . The bears sleep rather lightly.' That's something I need to remember." My students looked at me wide-eyed. "What are you thinking? Turn to your neighbor and talk."

After a few minutes, I inquired, "What are you thinking so far?" As they shared, I wrote their responses on a sticky note on my copy of the text (see Figure 7.6).

"Thanks for sharing. Let's go on. Don't forget to jot down your thinking—especially the ways it might be changing," I reminded them.

I read out loud and then jotted my thinking next to the second section (see Figure 7.7).

Again I invited students to share their thinking with the people around them and then with the rest of the group. "Remember, we're trying to figure out how synthesis helps us when we're reading a test passage. Now what are you thinking?" (See Figure 7.8.)

After Chauncey shared, "Now I'm thinking about all hibernators," I thought to myself, *Now they are getting it. Adding those bricks. They are beginning to see the power of synthesizing as test takers.*

"Boys and girls, I love what Chauncey just said. Did you hear that language of synthesis? We've been listening for language like that . . . *Now I'm thinking.*" I stepped away from the passage and added the words *Now I'm thinking . . .* to our ongoing chart of the language of synthesis.

When I looked at the clock, I realized we'd used ample crafting time. I knew we weren't finished with the article, but students weren't ready to read the rest of it independently. I decided instead that we'd return to it the next day.

"Boys and girls, I think we'll stop here for today—you need plenty of time to compose as readers. Here's what we'll do. Tomorrow for crafting, we'll come back to this piece and add to our thinking. Any last thoughts?"

"I'm thinking about hibernation differently now. It's not just about bears," Hannah said.

"I want to see if my thinking changes any more," Chauncey added.

"I want to know why it's called 'The Deep Sleepers,'" Chase contributed.

"It sounds just like a story, and I thought it was supposed to be an article," Daniel said with his usual smile.

"I can tell we have more thinking to do," I said. "Today as readers, you might want to think about this notion of synthesizing in your own reading. Tomorrow we'll take a look at this piece as test takers and see if synthesis helps us answer the questions."

As students went off to read independently, I spent a few minutes looking over the notes they'd jotted on their copies of the article. This helped me clarify the next day's craft lesson. It showed me which students tried to grapple with synthesizing an unfamiliar text.

What did I discover?

- Students were beginning to understand the process of synthesis.
- Many students still needed shared experiences to solidify their ability to synthesize independently.
- Students needed continued experiences with a wide variety of texts.
- We needed to continue to explore the important question, "How does synthesis help me as a test taker?"

We continued our look at synthesizing as test takers the following day. I began our craft lesson with an overview of our previous day's work so we could pick up this exploration where we had left off. To synthesize as test takers, it was important for students to see the outcome of their efforts over time. The following examples are from our second look at "Deep Sleepers" (see Figure 7.9).

Figure 7.9. This work shows the ways students continued their thinking in a second crafting session. Before they even saw the questions that followed the passage, they talked about their evolving thinking.

Now I'm thinking...
• Ground squirrels are able to slow down their breathing and heartbeat by 295 beats. They lower their body temperature by 60°... Hibernation must be about slowing down.

I'm thinking animals have very unique body systems.

When autumn comes, the ground squirrel digs a little burrow three feet under the ground. The temperature will always be the same there, even if it is freezing up above. The squirrel crawls into its little hole and rolls up into a tight ball. Ever so slowly, its heartbeat begins to slow down. It goes from 300 beats a minute to just five! The squirrel's body temperature falls from 95°F to 35°F. If our body temperature fell sixty degrees, it would kill us. Nobody knows how the ground squirrel can do this, but it works every time.

26   Level C

GO ON

What I'm thinking now...
• Not all animals hibernate the same. Some have different habits. Body temperature seems important to the process of hibernating.

Many other animals go into this deep sleep. The woodchuck, for example, also hibernates. Some bats hibernate, but they don't sleep through the whole winter. Bats can't let themselves get too hot or too cold. If they get too hot, they will use up their food too fast. If they get too cold, they will die. Sometimes bats have to wake up and move to another spot.

Hibernation is a big mystery. Scientists are not sure just how animals do it. But they would like to find out. If we could learn to hibernate, long space trips would not bother us. Just like the ground squirrel, we could sleep through the tough part.

Finally I'm thinking...

Hibernation is still something we don't fully understand and need to learn more about. We have a lot to learn for the future.

GO ON

Level C 27

- We can't store food like other animals. C.M.
- I'm still wondering about bears. H.B.
- What is the tough part? J.B.
- Scientists are thinking about how animals do it. B.F.
- I'm thinking I couldn't hibernate! J.M.

- How does the body temperature drop that far? C.N.
- Maybe the colder it gets the lower the temperature gets. C.M.
- Maybe their fat storage helps them lower their body temperature. J.B.
- Maybe the outside is cold, but the inside is warm. C.M.

- Now I'm thinking about bats and why they <u>move</u> so much. P.A.
- What other animals hibernate... T.A.
- I just found out that bats hibernate. S.B.
- I'm asking questions about bats. M.H.
- Now I'm thinking bats and bears are misunderstood. D.H.

Figure 7.9 *continued*

Naming How Our Thinking Evolves . . . Synthesis with Eighth-Grade Writers

By Missy Matthews

Two weeks of the school year had passed when I went to meet Lesli Cochran's new eighth-grade language arts students. The mysteries of scheduling had left this class out of balance. Based on previous standardized texts, only seven out of the twenty-eight students were considered proficient readers and writers. Lesli used every minute of her ninety-eight-minute block to keep them actively engaged with varying genres and meaningful topics. As students entered, Lesli introduced me and gave a brief description of our work for the day.

I started with the question, "What can you tell me about synthesis?" Blank stares glazed across student faces.

Finally, Karmin saved us from the silence. "Doesn't it have something to do with thinking about your writing? Like, when you have an assignment and you really have to think about it."

I turned Karmin's question back out to the group. "I don't know. What do you guys think?"

Silence filled the room once again. Dennis began, "Well, it has something to do with putting your background knowledge together with new knowledge to answer a question."

I could tell this conversation was going to need some help. These students had studied synthesis across their middle school careers, but since they came from different sixth- and seventh-grade teams, the depth and duration of their study had probably varied. Plus, it was only the third week of school, and we all know what happens to previously learned knowledge across the eternity of summer vacation.

I said, "I hear the word *synthesis* in *photosynthesis*. Have you heard that term before?" Enlightened looks replaced the blank stares.

A voice from the back of the room shared, "That has something to do with how plants get energy."

Karmin added, "Yeah, it's like how they use the sun's energy."

I nodded and paraphrased, "So photosynthesis has something to do with how plants use the sun's energy to eat."

Joey clarified, "They take the sun's energy and change it into food or their own energy." Finally, the word I was looking for: *change.*

"Have you ever heard of synthetic fibers?" I asked.

Zach said, "Yeah, it's like microfibers."

I pushed on. "In a factory that makes synthetics, they use different kinds of fibers to make something new. The original fibers are changed into a new kind of synthetic fiber. In those two examples, is there something you hear in common?"

"Change," Emily said.

"Yes, that's what synthesis is. It's a process of change.

"Let me show you how I synthesize as I work through a testing sample. Please take a test packet and gather around so we can talk about our work."

As the students gathered on the floor and in the closest desks around the overhead projector, their typical routine for whole-group instruction, I projected the released writing item onto the whiteboard.

"This first page says 'Written Composition.' That's what I'd expect a cover page for a writing test booklet to look like. And here on the second page, I see a box at the top with the words 'Write a composition about your favorite memory.' I think that's the prompt this test is asking me to write about. And down here at the bottom of the page, I see this other box with things I should remember to include in my writing. I notice specific words in those sentences like *detail, correct spelling and punctuation,* and *clear ideas.* The test makers must be telling me what they think is important. I'll need to keep these ideas in mind, so that I can make sure I've included them in my writing.

"The next page in the packet is the prewriting page. I don't know if this is something I have to do, but I know on some tests, you actually get points for planning. I'm going to make sure to show that I've planned just in case. The next page is just empty lines. That must be where I'm supposed to do the actual writing.

"As I look at page four in the packet, I notice my thinking changing, or a place where I am synthesizing. Do you see how the format of the test has changed? I was thinking about how my work would be to plan and compose a piece of writing. Now I'm thinking my work will also include finding punctuation, spelling, capitalization, and grammar errors in multiple-choice questions. That's different from what I initially envisioned.

"I'm going to stop thinking aloud now and record some of my ideas."

On a long piece of butcher paper I drew a time line and titled it "A Timeline of Our Thinking" (see Figure 7.10).

"At the beginning of my work, I was thinking about the written composition. I knew I was actually going to write and that my writing was going to be about a favorite memory."

I recorded "Written Composition: I'm going to actually write" on the far left side of the time line.

I continued on. "When I came to the revising and editing section, which was all multiple choice, my thinking changed. I knew I would have to choose correct answers instead of writing."

I added to the time line "Revising & Editing: Now this is multiple choice."

"I can label this thinking as synthesis, because there was a change in the way I was thinking about my work as a test taker. Before you get started on your own, are there initial thoughts you want me to put on this time line?"

Joey said, "I don't like this, and I'm bad at it."

"Is this for a grade?" Tanner asked.

Karmin chimed in, "I think writing tests are lame, because they aren't about what we're learning in school."

Bernice added, "Why do there have to be so many sections?"

"Do we really have to do this test?" Ryan asked.

"Yes, you really do have to do this test," I answered. "But instead of the answers being the most important thing today, your thinking is what matters. So here's what we're going to do. Here's a stack of sticky notes. Head off to your desk and work on this written composition section. You'll have about twenty minutes. When I call you back to the group, bring your sticky notes and test packet, and we'll add to our time line of thinking. I'll see you back here in twenty minutes."

Students went to their desks, and I could feel the energy drain from the room. This was not the typical work they had come to expect from this class.

Figure 7.10

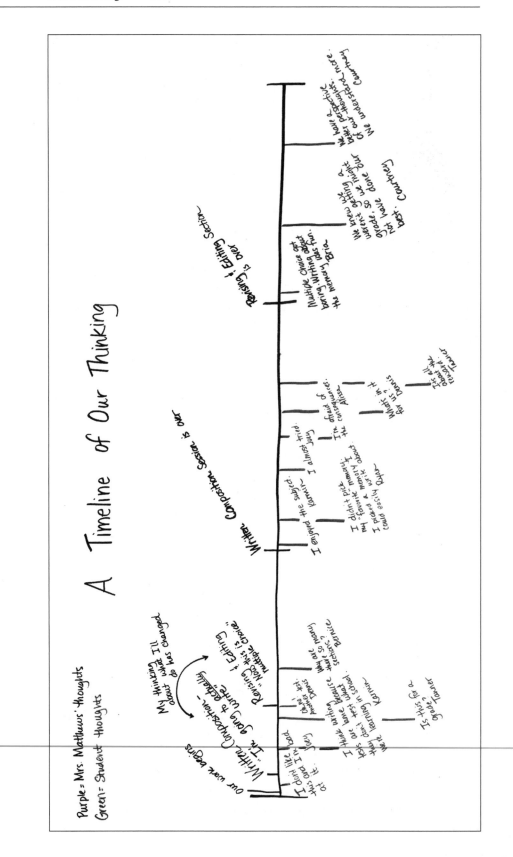

Marley immediately flagged me down, so I pulled up a chair and began to confer with her first.

"I don't know how to plan. What does that mean? I didn't go to this school last year, and I don't know what a plan is," she began, panic in her voice.

"In your classes at your other school, did you ever have to show how you were thinking about your writing before you did the writing?" I asked.

"No."

I knew this wasn't really the place to go into detail about planning, but I added it to my list of things to share with Lesli and decided to share a couple of quick ideas that Marley could use with little instruction.

"As a writer, there are a lot of different ways I plan for my writing. Sometimes I use a list to generate ideas I want to include about a topic. If I were writing about my son, Kyle, I could make a list of all the things he says that make me laugh. Or I could make some kind of web to show my thinking. I might write my topic in the center of the page and draw lines out to different ideas I want to include about the topic. It might look something like this." I drew a generic web in my notebook to show her.

Marley looked much less stressed about this task. I asked, "Do you think you have enough to get started?" She nodded. "Okay, I'm going to leave you to your work."

After this conference, I wanted to get a sense of what students were up to. I made a lap around the classroom to look over shoulders and hear the buzz of conversation.

I noticed Matt sitting with his arms crossed and intently not making eye contact with me. I pulled up beside him and said, "What are you thinking about this work, Matt?"

"I'm not," he replied.

"What do you mean?" I asked.

"I don't know what to do," Matt said.

At this point I noticed a sticky note where he had recorded his thinking. It read, "This is boring, it is hard, I am afraid to fail." I asked Matt to share his thinking about the sticky note.

"I don't know what to do," he said.

"I'm so interested in what you've written here. One of the things I wonder about is how our feelings about tests affect how well we do on them. What's something you love to do?"

"Play video games."

"Do you ever say to yourself, 'I don't think I'm going to play well today'?"

"No."

"Why not?" I asked.

"Because when I'm playing a video game, it doesn't matter if I die. I just start the game over," Matt said.

"So, on a test, you can't just do it over, can you?"

"No."

"I'm wondering if your concern about not doing well gets in your way of even trying. Here's what I want us to do. Let's see if we can just get started. If I can see what you're thinking as a writer, it will really help me understand how we can figure this out."

Matt shrugged.

"On this page, the test maker wants you to plan your writing. On many tests, you can get points for just putting something down on the planning sheet. As long as it shows the grader you're attempting the prompt, you can get points. Since you love video games, tell me a favorite memory of one of them."

"It's the same every day. My friends come over and bug me while I play," Matt said.

"The grader isn't going to know if your memory really happened the way you describe. My suggestion is to think of a time you were playing and having a great time. Pick a memory where the details are very clear in your mind. That way, you can include those in what you write. Remember, you're being tested on how well you can craft a piece. Use all you know about great writing. I'm going to go talk with some other students. I want you to give this a shot, and we'll see how it goes. Sound like a plan?"

Matt agreed, and I headed off with my notebook.

After a few minutes of peering over shoulders to see how students were doing, I called them back to the gathering area. I wrote on the time line "Written Composition Session is over."

"How's it going?" I said.

"I enjoyed the subject of the prompt," Karmin shared. "It was something outside of school I could write about."

"That's interesting to me, Karmin. I can tell that's a place where your thinking has changed, or you've synthesized. See here at the beginning of our time line? You said that writing tests are lame, and here you've discovered a place that was enjoyable. When you got into the test, your thinking changed. That's synthesis," I said.

Ryan said, "I didn't pick my favorite memory like the prompt says, but I did choose a memory I could easily write about. My thinking is different about how I use the prompt."

"That's synthesis," I said. "Your thinking as a test taker is different now from what it was when you started. And I think what you did was very smart. It's more important to choose a memory you know you can write about well than to limit yourself to a favorite. The test maker really won't know the difference.

"Joey, what are you thinking?" I probed, knowing Joey would have a lot to say.

"I almost tried," he said.

"Tell me what you mean. What made you almost want to try?" I was interested in the *almost* part of this statement. I knew it wasn't interesting to these students, but I wondered if I could get him to tell me what might be worth his effort.

"I thought I might be able to write about a memory."

"If you think you can do well, are you motivated to try?"

"It's not really motivated, but maybe willing," Joey responded.

Alissa chimed in, "But I'm afraid of the consequences."

"What consequences are there for trying?" I wondered aloud.

"I could be wrong," Alissa answered. "I'm afraid of the consequences."

Dennis shared, "Yeah, and what's in it for us?"

You could hear the rumblings around the room in response to Dennis's question.

Tanner said, "What's our reward?"

I was struck by their questions, and the obvious agreement of their classmates.

"What would happen if you almost tried on your driver's test?" I said.

Tanner said, "I wouldn't almost try."

"Why not?" I asked.

"Because that matters to me. There's a bad consequence if I don't do well."

"Okay, what about your ACT or SAT? What if you *almost* tried on those?"

Tanner continued, "I'd try hard on those, because if I do well, I can get into the college I want to go to. But if I don't, I may have to go to some little college I don't want to go to. That matters."

"But CSAP doesn't matter to you?" I asked.

"That's just for the teachers," Courtney shared.

I knew the focus of our work was supposed to be on synthesis, but I couldn't help it. I wanted to hear their thoughts.

I recorded their comments on our time line and said, "Let's go ahead and work on the second part of our test and see where our thinking leads. The next part is multiple choice. Give it a go and I'll check in with you shortly."

Students went back to their seats and began to work. I had noticed Abby's body language during the class period. She seemed frustrated and possibly angry, so I made sure to confer with her next. She hadn't written anything on the composition part of the test, but she had completed all of the multiple-choice questions.

"Abby, I'm really curious about your work today. Help me understand why you did the second section first."

"I know I can do multiple-choice problems," she explained. "I've seen a lot of those before. But I don't understand what to do on the writing part, so I'm not going to do it."

"So, you're much more comfortable with the second section because that's a familiar testing format for you," I said.

Abby added, "Yes. I'm not comfortable with the first part of the test, because I don't understand what they want from me."

"That makes sense to me. So how is synthesis playing a role in the work you're doing? How is your thinking changing?"

"Maybe I can try the planning page," Abby said.

"It sounds like your thinking has changed. You didn't want to try the written composition at first, but after hearing from some of your classmates, you may be ready to try."

Abby nodded.

"Abby, I want to make sure you record this thinking. When you saw the first part of the test, you didn't know what to do. But when you came to the multiple-choice section, you felt more comfortable because it was familiar. Would you please jot a note on a sticky for each section so we can remember the ways your thinking changed?"

Abby agreed and began to write. I made a few notes myself. Across the room, I noticed Matt was writing, so instead of checking back in with him, I left him alone.

After two more conferences, I could tell the students were at the limit of their stamina. They'd played along with me for as long as they possibly could. I asked them to join me to reflect.

I walked to our time line and waited for the students to get themselves settled. "What can you tell me about your thinking now?"

"The multiple choice got boring. Writing about a memory was fun," Bria offered.

"Did you notice how you were synthesizing?" I asked.

She continued, "I guess I just realized that when I can actually write, I do a better job than when I have to pick answers. I used to think multiple choice was the easiest part of a test, but now I know I can show my writing better when I like the topic. The grader will know who I am as a writer."

Courtney shared her idea, "I think that since we weren't getting a grade for this, we might not have done our best. But at least now we have a different perspective and we understand more about how we think on tests."

"I hope that has happened for you today," I said. "Before you leave, let me share a few of the things I've learned from you today." I opened my notebook and read some of the notes I had jotted down. Sharing these notes was my way of honoring the important lessons the students had taught me.

After the students left, Lesli and her teammates joined me. I thumbed through the students' papers and found Matt's. After our conference, Matt had attempted the test's planning page. He had created a list:

- riding a bike
- tire gets flat but you still ride it
- your tires get bald

Not only had Matt decided to give the test a try, but he planned to write about a topic other than the one we'd talked about in our conference. I couldn't help but feel that we'd cracked open a door that had once been locked.

As much as I want to say that students left this lesson having a much deeper understanding of the ways synthesis works when they're engaged in testing materials, I can't. Certainly, we began the discussion. There were places I was able to label their thinking as synthesis. And at times, they were able to do it, too. But synthesis happened in a greater way. It was my own. The clarity of my thinking about this work with older students had evolved.

Every time I tackled the idea of thinking through tests with older students, something was different. I began to think over and over, "They have more history with testing." But it wasn't until my conference with Matt that I clearly understood the effect of that history.

I've yet to hear a third grader say, "I don't want to do this work because I'm afraid to fail." Not only did Matt say it, but he wrote it, and he believed it. More important, he's not the only one. His experience with testing tells him that failure is a possibility. On this day, Matt's words spoke for many of his peers who have taken standardized tests, received no feedback, and been told by a single phrase on a results sheet that they didn't meet the standard. That history makes this work different for older students.

My new thinking came when Dennis said, "What's in it for me?" I've spent the last couple of days pondering that question. What is in it for students? I can name what's in it for them when they take their ACT or SAT. I can name what's in it for them when they take their driver's license test. So why is showing their thinking and learning on a state test important to them? I'm not sure.

I am sure that relevance and purpose, or the lack thereof, around testing greatly affects older students. We have to build their confidence for this kind of work, change their preconceived notions that they are at the mercy of the test, and name the ways their brilliant thinking allows them to show who they are on testing day.

POSSIBILITIES: Craft Lessons for Synthesizing New Learnings and Ideas

When we're taking tests, what words signal that we'll need to synthesize?
> Collect the words and phrases test makers use to suggest that synthesizing would be an effective strategy to employ. (E.g., "What would be the best title for this story/graph/outline/etc.?" "What lesson did the main character learn?")

How does paying attention to the ways our thinking evolves help us stay grounded when we're taking a test?
> List advantages of maintaining a running synthesis throughout a test passage or section. (E.g., "First I thought this problem about fencing a pasture involved figuring out the area, but as I read on, I'm thinking it's actually about finding perimeter. Now I know which formula to choose.")

When there's a multistep or multipart question on a test, how does synthesis help us?
> Recognize when a previous answer or previous thinking is necessary for completing the next step or second part of a test item. (E.g., "In Part A I had to draw a bracelet using a specific pattern. Now Part B is asking me to use my answer to draw a necklace that is eighteen inches long.")

When we have to construct a written explanation, how do we synthesize what we know about content, process, and conventions to make our ideas clear?
> Name the ways learners weave various threads of information together. (E.g., "I've got to use everything I know about writing a lab report to complete this section on the science test.")

How would we use synthesis to make sense of this material if we found it outside a testing situation?
> Compare ways synthesis supports meaning making in various contents and contexts. (E.g., "Normally, I'd reread poems several times to figure out what they mean. But in a testing situation, I don't think I'd have that kind of time. I'd need to get to deeper themes in the first or second read.")

Activate, Utilize, and Build Background Knowledge (Schema)

Making connections, building bridges between old and new, opening mental files—we've used these metaphors to show how our prior knowledge and experiences affect our capacity to understand new ideas. When we know a lot about something, new learning is easier. When our file folder on a particular subject is thin or empty, new learning is a great deal more challenging. It's easy for a football fan to make sense of a Rick Reilly essay about the plight of football fanatics when the dark days of February roll around and the next preseason game is six months away. It's a different story for those who view Sundays, August through January, as television wasteland.

When faced with a test, using background knowledge takes on a new look. To level the playing field, so to speak, evaluators look to measure what test takers understand about the actual content presented. Applying everything you know about building picnic tables to a test passage about building picnic tables may actually do more harm than good.

Therefore, test takers . . .

- apply what they know about different testing formats. ("I know reading tests usually have a question or two at the end of a section that has me compare ideas from all the earlier passages. I'm going to have to remember all the stories as I go along to make that part easier.")
- use what they know about tests to be ready for confusing or tricky items. ("There are always a couple of close answers on these math multiple-choice tests.")
- build and refine their schema within and across testing experiences. ("Last year I had plenty of time at the end of the first day of writing. This year, I'll try to use any extra time to go back over what I've written to check for silly mistakes.")

- suspend irrelevant or incorrect schema and rely on passage-specific information. ("Wait a minute. This asks about the highest mountain in North America, but it doesn't have Mount McKinley as one of the choices. I'm sure that's the right answer because I did a research paper on it last year. I better go back and find what the article says before I choose an answer.")

- use known testing vocabulary, such as *describe, explain, summarize,* to help them decide what sort of answer the evaluator is expecting. ("It says I'm supposed to compare the two main characters from the two stories I've already read. I know that in a testing situation, the word *compare* means to tell what's the same *and* what's different.")

- make sense of complex test vocabulary based on their previous knowledge of derivatives, prefixes, and suffixes. ("That prefix means . . . , so that word must mean . . .")

Student Examples—Naming What They Notice About Tests and Using Background Knowledge

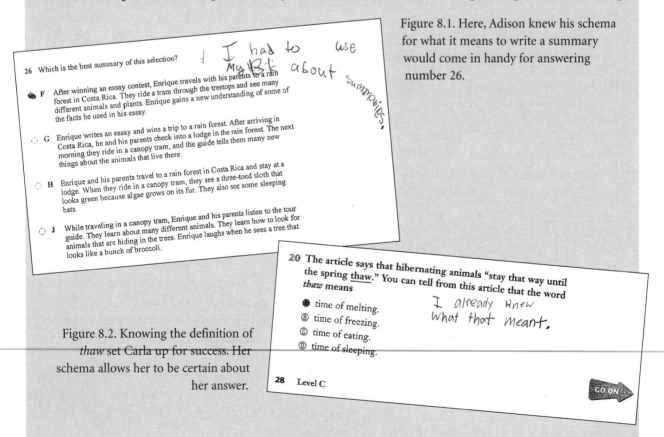

Figure 8.1. Here, Adison knew his schema for what it means to write a summary would come in handy for answering number 26.

Figure 8.2. Knowing the definition of *thaw* set Carla up for success. Her schema allows her to be certain about her answer.

Student Examples—Naming What They Notice About Tests and Using Background Knowledge

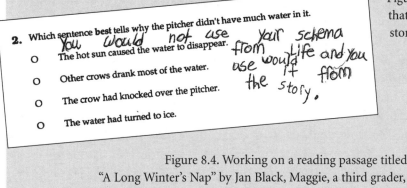

2. Which sentence best tells why the pitcher didn't have much water in it.

You would not use your schema from life and you use would it from the story.

○ The hot sun caused the water to disappear.

○ Other crows drank most of the water.

○ The crow had knocked over the pitcher.

○ The water had turned to ice.

Figure 8.3. Marc, Armon, and Ruyee realize that the answer will have to come from the story, not from their life experiences.

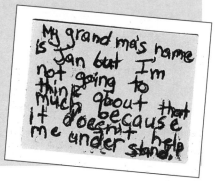

My grand ma's name is Jan but I'm not going to think much about that because it doesn't help me understand.

Figure 8.4. Working on a reading passage titled "A Long Winter's Nap" by Jan Black, Maggie, a third grader, demonstrates her ability to separate relevant from irrelevant schema.

STORIES FROM THE CLASSROOM

Launching an Investigation into the Link Between Background Knowledge and Tests

By Lori L. Conrad

Angel Wolf's fourth graders had been learning about the ways successful readers and writers activate and build their schema for three weeks. They'd discovered that readers make different kinds of connections while they read:

- Sometimes the links are between what they're reading and what they've already experienced.
- Sometimes the links are between what they're reading and another text in their reading history.
- Sometimes the links are between what they're reading and knowledge they have about the world around them.

Across all these conversations, they'd come to know that some connections are worthwhile because they further understanding—and others don't matter much and need to be ignored because they do more to distract a reader's thinking than anything else.

As writers, the class had worked to compose memoirs—texts that told the stories of their lives. They'd discovered that memoir writing was a perfect way to share their schema.

On this day, I joined the ongoing study hoping to extend the initial thinking to include tests. As the class gathered on the rug in the center of the room, I began by asking, "What have you already figured out about the ways successful thinkers use schema?"

Hands shot up. Sitting at the back edge of the gathering spot, Angel looked up from her notebook and smiled. She knew the kids would have a lot to say.

"We use our BK [background knowledge] to help us understand our reading. If we know a lot, if we have a lot of BK, then the reading is easier," Anthony began.

"Background knowledge is what we already know about the book or our own experience or about someone's ideas," Kamren added.

I started a new anchor chart so I'd have a place to capture this thinking (see Figure 8.5).

Figure 8.5

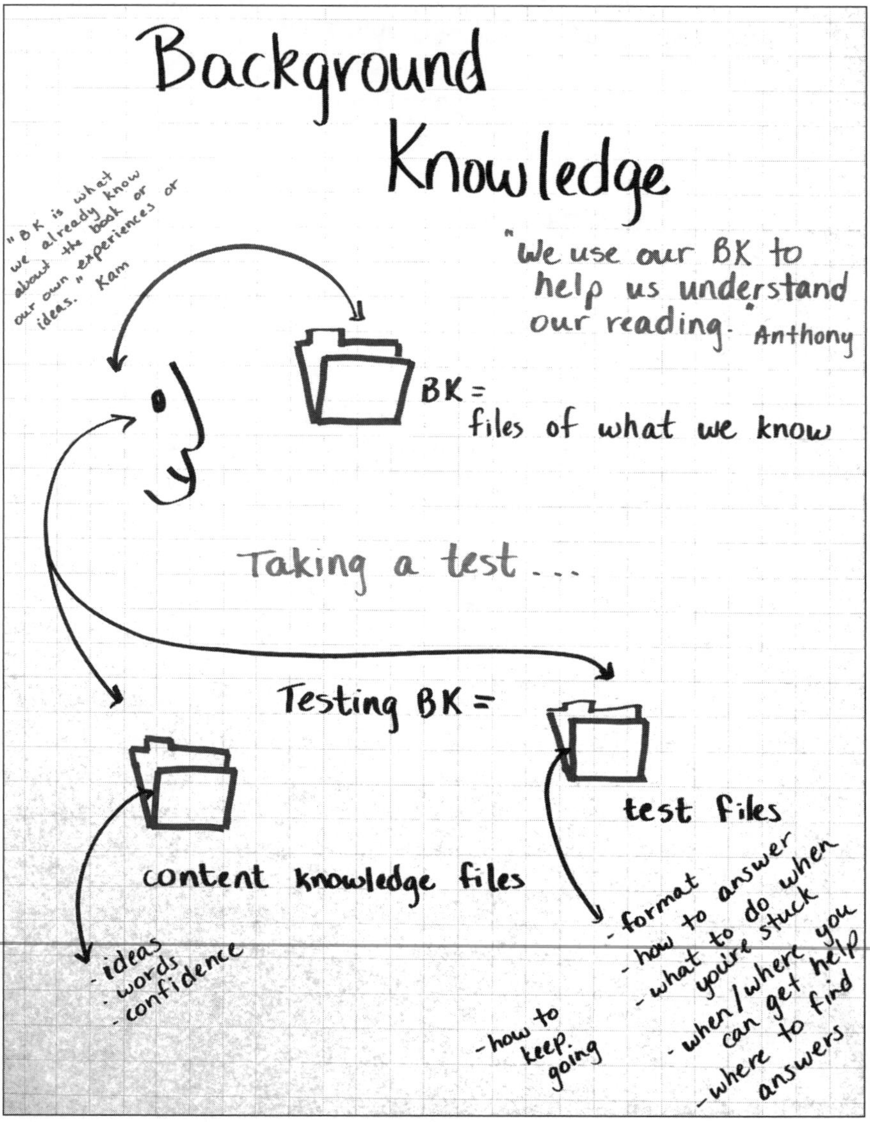

Background Knowledge

"BK is what we already know about the book or our own experiences or ideas." Kam

"We use our BK to help us understand our reading." Anthony

BK = files of what we know

Taking a test...

Testing BK =

test files
- format to answer
- how to do when you're stuck
- what to answer when
- when/where you can get help
- where to find answers

content knowledge files
- ideas
- words
- confidence

- how to keep going

"Today, I'd like to stretch what you've already figured out about schema. I'm trying to figure out how BK works when I'm taking a test. My hypothesis is that sometimes smart test takers have to open the mental file that contains information about the content of the test. Like, if I'm taking a test on multiplication, it makes sense for me to open my 'multiplication file' so I can do what Anthony said and use my BK to help me understand.

"But I'm also thinking I might have to open a file I'll call 'what I know about tests.' This is the file where I keep my schema about how tests are set up and what test takers have to do to show how smart they are.

"I want you all to be researchers—and my research question is this: When are you using your mental file about the content of the test, and when are you using your mental file for the way tests are set up?"

With nods of agreement, the group of nine- and ten-year-old researchers shuffled through examples of released test items I'd brought with me to class that day. Some chose the science sample about soil erosion. Others picked the nonfiction reading sample about whales. A few chose the writing prompt. The last couple tried their hand at the math sample picturing the back of a cereal box accompanied by a few questions.

As the fourth graders headed to their seats to tackle their test samples, I sat down to confer with Carter.

He'd selected the science example and was busy reading the first page to himself. The test presented a science investigation into soil erosion. Carter had underlined part of the first sentence: "<u>After a rain storm, Margo saw a lot of soil on the sidewalks.</u>" He knew that I'd be curious about what he was doing, so he began.

"I've seen when soil floods over the sidewalk after it rains. That makes a strong image in my mind."

"I know what you mean . . . Rain can make a real mess. How do you think this connection with your schema will help you understand the rest of the test?" I asked.

Carter looked puzzled. "I don't know. I know I'm using my content file, but I guess I need to keep reading to decide whether this is going to help me get the questions right."

"When we come back to the carpet to reflect, I'd love for you to share this thinking with the rest of the class," I said, jotting Carter's words down in my notebook.

As I moved to the next table, I noticed that Jacob was in the middle of the math sample.

"How's it going, Jacob?"

"On the first page I underlined some of the stuff they printed on the box," he said, turning back to the first page that included a picture of a cereal box (Figure 8.6). "Then I wrote this on a sticky note: 'I think some of this info on the box is false.' Then, when I got to the questions, I started filling in

Figure 8.6

the bubbles. I figured out that's how I'd show the test makers which answers I picked."

"By the way you say that, I'm not convinced you think that's going to work all the time. When would that not work?" I asked.

Jacob flipped to the end of the test. "Here at the end, when there's room for writing. Then I know they want more than just picking the right answer."

"Hmm. I can see how you're using your knowledge about advertisements and your knowledge of making sense of tests," I noted. "Be ready to share some of this when we gather back together."

As I stepped away from Jacob, Molly tugged on my sleeve. "I took the test about breakfast cereal and I want to change," she said. "I don't really have any schema for this kind of cereal and I don't really read boxes, so can I take a different test?"

"That is an interesting question, Molly. I know that picking your own reading material is something you guys do all the time here in Mrs. Wolf's room, and I know that you all have agreed that if a book is wrong for you, it's okay to abandon it and pick something else to read. But today, I'm going to ask that you keep working on this test sample. I want to hear what you figure out about taking a test when you either don't like the topic or don't have much background knowledge about it."

Molly agreed and headed back to her desk. Angel and I jotted this conversation down in our notes. We both knew it was something we'd need to address during a later lesson with the whole class.

Emily chose the writing subtest. She'd already jotted down a few lines on the first page containing the actual directions, erased those, and moved on to the page meant for her answers.

"Emily, I notice that you did a bunch of erasing on the first page. Tell me what you're thinking."

"Well, I read writing task number one and thought about something I had already written. But then I realized that I didn't have enough room to tell all about the time Molly stuck up for me. I remembered that writing tests include a specific place for us to write. So when I found the place with all the lines, I had to go back and erase what I had written first. I knew the test people wouldn't even read that part. They'd only read the part on the answer lines."

"That's so smart," I said as I wrote her thinking down in my notes. "Be sure to bring that example along to the carpet."

As we gathered back together, it became clear that our mental file about tests included such things as test structures, answer formats, what to do when we get stuck, where we get help when things don't make sense, where to find specific answers, and how to keep going even when we get bored. Our content-knowledge file included words and ideas about the subject being tested as well as the confidence we had about that subject (see Figure 8.7a–8.7d).

But two interesting questions surfaced for a number of the fourth graders:

1. What do I do when my background knowledge is different from the information included on the test?
2. What happens when I rely on my schema, and not so much on the test, when it comes time to answer the questions?

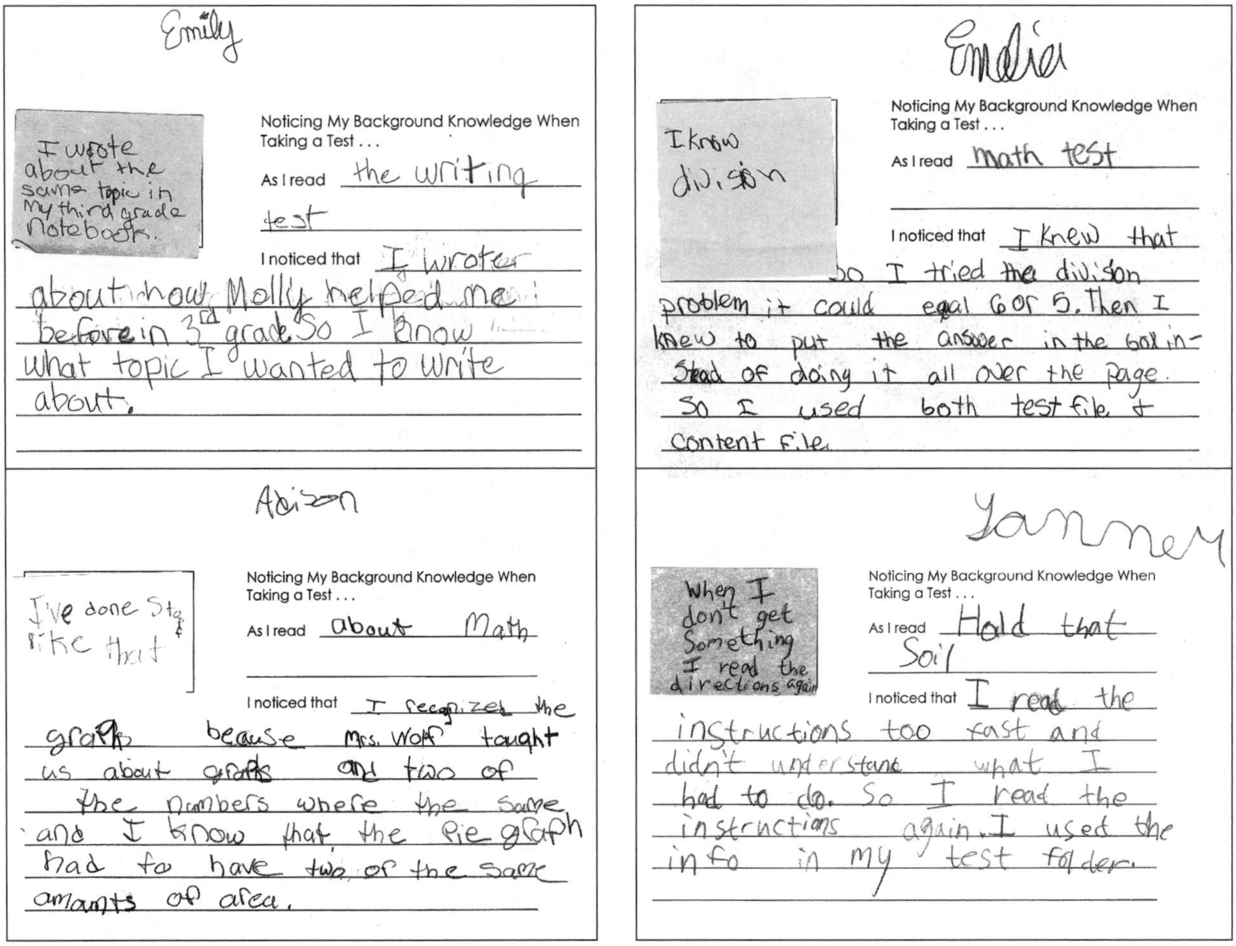

Emily

Noticing My Background Knowledge When Taking a Test . . .

As I read   the writing test

I wrote about the same topic in my third grade notebook.

I noticed that   I wrote about how Molly helped me before in 3rd grade so I know what topic I wanted to write about.

Emelia

Noticing My Background Knowledge When Taking a Test . . .

As I read   math test

I know division

I noticed that   I knew that so I tried the division problem it could eqal 6 or 5. Then I knew to put the answer in the box instead of doing it all over the page. So I used both test file + content file.

Adison

Noticing My Background Knowledge When Taking a Test . . .

As I read   about Math

I've done stf like that

I noticed that   I recognized the graph because Mrs. Wolf taught us about graphs and two of the numbers where the same and I know that the pie graph had to have two of the same amounts of area.

Tanner

Noticing My Background Knowledge When Taking a Test . . .

As I read   Hold that Soil

When I don't get something I read the directions again

I noticed that   I read the instructions too fast and didn't understand what I had to do. So I read the instructions again. I used the info in my test folder.

Figure 8.7a–d

Angel and I quickly decided on a couple of lessons she'd teach before I returned the following week:

1. How does a reader and smart test taker know to "let go" of a connection that isn't proving to be helpful? (following up on the questions raised during Carter's conference)
2. What does a reader and test taker do when she has no schema for the content being tested? (following up on the issue raised during Molly's conference)

When I returned a few days later and invited the kids to come to the carpet and tell me what they'd been working on, they couldn't wait to share all that they'd figured out.

"We talked a lot about what to do when you're taking a test and you don't have any schema," Molly began. "You just fake it and really use what's in the test."

George looked at the test. It said:

Rabbits eat:

☐ lettuce

☐ dog food

☐ sandwiches

He raised his hand.

"Rabbits have to eat carrots, or their teeth will get too long and stick into them," he said.

The teacher nodded and smiled, but she put her finger to her lips. George carefully drew in a carrot so the test people would know.

Figure 8.8

"Yeah, we don't get to ask for another one," Drew agreed.

"We also figured out that you can't know if your BK will help until you get to the questions. Sometimes it doesn't matter at all because the questions ask for different things," Ivy added.

"Today, I'm going to push a little harder," I said. "Test makers write these things for loads of fourth graders. They don't really know, or even care, about what you're learning here with Mrs. Wolf. When they write a test, they have to create what's called a level playing field—so they write questions designed to figure out how well you understood their test and the content they think is important, not how much you know about the world. They want you to rely on what's in the test rather than what's in your head.

"Here's a book that shows what I mean. It's called *First Grade Takes a Test* by Miriam Cohen, and it's about a group of first graders who have to take a special test to show what they know. Here, listen to these pages . . ." (See Figure 8.8.)

"When I read this, at first I giggled. Then I realized this little kid was being too smart for the test. He was relying on what he knew about rabbits when he should have been choosing from what the test makers know about rabbits.

"Today, instead of letting you choose between a bunch of test samples, I've brought just one. It's a reading test for fourth graders, and it's written to see how well you guys can make sense of an informational passage about the Sacramento Zoo. I picked it because I knew you all would bring different background knowledge about zoos to the test.

"But before I let you head off to read, flip the test over and make a list of everything you already know about zoos—just a quick jot. When we're finished, we'll go back and decide whether the information on your list helped you make sense of the nonfiction passage or not."

The students busily listed the things they already knew about zoos. The lists included things such as the following:

- You should be careful.
- They don't kill their food in the zoo.
- I know that zookeepers set a special time for the feedings for the animals.
- You have to have the right food for the different animals.
- It would be cool to be a zookeeper.
- I fed a cub before.
- The zoo people usually go in their [the animals'] cages.
- Babies eat from a bottle or from their mothers.
- Zoo people feed tigers meat.

"Now that you've activated your schema about zoos, go ahead and read the passage. As you do, highlight anything in the passage you already knew. In about twenty minutes we'll come back together to share what we've figured out."

The fourth graders grabbed their highlighters and headed back to their seats. Once they settled in, I headed out to confer.

Jina, a girl new to the school, had a frustrated look on her face as I crouched beside her.

"What's going on? You look frustrated."

"I am," Jina said. "I've never been to a zoo. There wasn't one where I lived before, and we haven't gotten to this one yet. I don't think it's fair."

"I hear that. It can feel a little unfair when a test is asking you to read something you don't know much about. It's okay today because we're researching what we might do when this happens in a real test. So, don't worry. I'm just curious what your plan might be to get through this test."

"I guess I have to find all the answers in the test because there won't be any in my head."

"Jina, that's so smart to know as you start reading. You're not going to be able to rely on anything other than the print they gave you. I can't wait to hear what you figure out when we gather back together."

Moving on, I noticed that Tanner had "that look"—he wanted my attention.

"I highlighted the part here that says 'the refrigerator and freezer are big enough to walk into,' he said. "I once asked a guy at the zoo where they kept all the food for the tigers. But I have to wait 'til I get to the questions to know if this BK helps or not."

"I'll be curious to hear what you decide."

Drew raised his hand and motioned me over to his table.

"What's up?" I asked.

"I read all the questions already and there isn't one about walruses. On my list I wrote down that I already knew that walruses eat salmon. So that schema isn't going to help me at all, is it?" he said.

"It doesn't sound like it."

"So I better ignore it, right?"

"That makes sense to me. I can't wait for you to share that when we get back together. We'll add that to our chart."

After a few more minutes, I invited everyone to join me on the carpet. "Mrs. Wolf and I are beginning to figure a few things out. It seems that sometimes your schema matches what's on the test, and when this happens, your schema helps you make sense of the words and ideas included on the test. But sometimes your schema doesn't match the test and can actually distract you from your job of understanding. I'm going to make another chart to record this new learning" (see Figure 8.9).

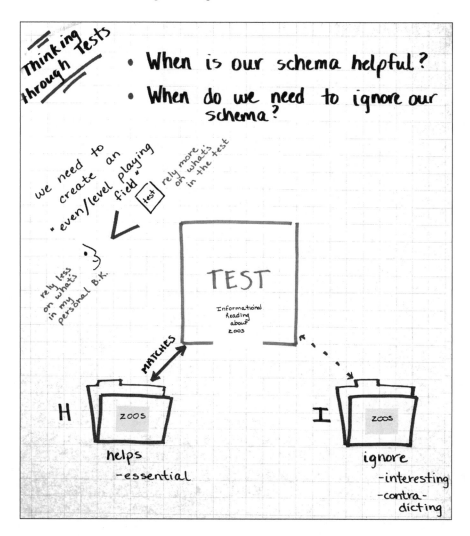

Figure 8.9

"Now, go back to that initial list you jotted on the back of the test. As you reread it, decide whether having that schema helped you make sense of the test passage or helped you answer the questions. Put an *H* beside each of those jots. Code anything from your initial list that actually didn't matter or didn't help you with an *I* because it's just interesting to know."

Patrick decided that knowing zookeepers had to put the animals in the cages before they could put the food out was helpful schema. Maureen figured out that her knowledge of zoo food really helped because she expected words such as *vitamins, zoo kitchen, healthy, meat,* and *plants* to show up in the passage. Monica thought that having actually been to the Sacramento Zoo was especially helpful because she could remember visiting some of the places mentioned in the test. Carter believed his knowledge of how zoo animals' eating habits differ from wild animals' eating habits—zoo animals don't kill their food, they don't eat live food, and zookeepers need to give them the right kind of food, the kind they would eat in the wild—helped him make sense of the article.

Anthony figured out that his schema about not taunting zoo animals and not putting your hands in the animals' mouths wasn't really helpful because the article didn't talk about either idea. And Olivia realized that her list of animals and the foods she knew they ate didn't matter much because the article talked about different animals.

As Angel and I conferred, we learned a lot about how schema helps and hinders test takers. Through the students' insights, we were able to add these items to our anchor chart:

- Test takers need to know when to stop using their schema.
- Test takers can read the questions first to focus their reading attention, but they need to read and use what's in the test to answer the questions rather than answer them based on their schema alone.
- Sometimes test takers can't know if their schema will be helpful until they're finished answering all the test questions.

These two new anchor charts joined their previously composed counterparts on the back wall of the classroom below the big heading "ways we make sense of the word and the world."

POSSIBILITIES: Craft Lessons for Using Background Knowledge

What test words or phrases let us know when it's helpful to use our schema and when it's really important to use just what's written in the test?

List test-specific language that defines the source options for test takers. (E.g., "This question says, 'according to the author.' I know that means I can only use words and ideas from the test itself.")

How can we use what we know about scoring rubrics to help us compose more effective test answers?

Compare the types of rubrics and scoring guides used for typical classroom work with those used for standardized tests. (E.g., "I know the short answers I have to write for the math test will be scored differently from the writing I do for writer's workshop. My math answer will get points for the ideas; there aren't points for spelling and sentence fluency.")

Other than testing, when do we have to work within very specific time restraints?

Name activities where time is a critical element in proficient completion. (E.g., "When I play hockey and one of the other team's players gets sent to the penalty box, our team has to pay attention to the clock. It's in those couple of minutes that we have a big advantage. That's sort of like when a test maker gives us only ten minutes to complete a certain number of problems.")

To compose a really complete answer, when can we use our background knowledge "as is" and when do we need to modify it a bit to fit the question?

Note the different ways successful test takers adapt schema to fit a testing situation. (E.g., "For this writing prompt I'm supposed to write about my favorite place. I don't really have one, so I guess I'll have to write about a place I can describe well and just pretend it's my favorite.")

When would we naturally use our schema to make sense of this material if this wasn't meant specifically for a test?

Describe specific examples when students' background knowledge and experiences support ongoing understanding. (E.g., "I know all about the different ways to accurately present data. Sometimes a line graph makes sense, but other times a bar graph is more appropriate.")

Chapter 9
TEST TAKERS

Determine the Most Important Ideas and Themes

Whether deciding what clothes to pack for a weekend trip to the mountains or choosing which of the monthly bills to pay first, determining importance is an ongoing act of sifting and sorting. Determining importance is like draining the boiling water from a pot of macaroni: once cooked, only the noodles are important for making mac 'n' cheese.

Mathematicians working to solve complex problems are often faced with a myriad of facts. They need to decide which set of numbers is most necessary to consider, which algorithm is most appropriate, which solution would make the most sense given the situation. Being able to determine what's most important makes it possible for mathematicians to pay attention to the statistics that matter and ignore those that distract.

Standardized tests are often filled with extraneous information test takers have to sift through to score well. Time constraints, unnecessary detail, overly developed descriptions, and carefully placed "red herrings" tax a test taker's brain space.

Therefore, successful test takers are able to . . .

- find important words or sentences that indicate what they'll need to do to score well. ("This question asks me to explain the three things plants need to create oxygen. It's really helpful to know how many details I'll need to include in my answer.")
- determine what test information will be essential when answering questions and what information will not be pertinent. ("I know I'll need to compare the main characters from these two stories after I've finished reading. I better pay close attention to those characters. It's good to know I won't need to pay as much attention to the two story settings.")
- decide what to include and what to leave out of a response, depending on the test's prompts. ("There are four lines for my written response.

That really helps me determine how much I'll need to write." "Writing this short constructed response is a lot like doing a line lift in my writer's notebook. I'll just take a portion of the test prompt and use it as part of my first sentence.")

- discover places in the test from which questions are most likely to be drawn. ("These boldface words and definitions will probably be important. I bet there will be a question or two about this vocabulary later on in the test.")

- use test directions to help decide what's most important. ("It says I'm supposed to explain my thinking using examples from the passage, so I can't just tell what I think. I have to back it up with specific evidence from the test.")

- adjust their test-taking pace according to directions and time constraints. ("I have only eight minutes to read this section and answer the questions. I better skim it pretty quickly. That way I'll have time to go back and reread if I need to.")

- use the information presented on graphs, charts, or other visual representations to understand essential data. ("It would be stupid to skip this chart of highest and lowest spending ratios. Understanding the differences is obviously what this test section is all about.")

Student Examples—Naming What They Notice About Tests and Determining Importance

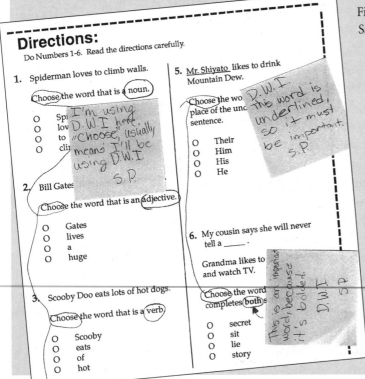

Figure 9.1. Throughout the questions, Samantha finds herself noticing key words.

Figure 9.2.
Simply stated, Sarah knows that the directions play a key role in any test.

Student Examples—Naming What They Notice About Tests and Determining Importance

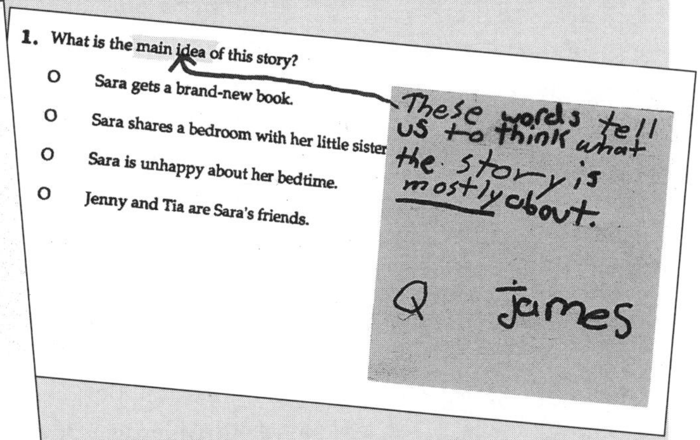
1. What is the main idea of this story?
O Sara gets a brand-new book.
O Sara shares a bedroom with her little sister
O Sara is unhappy about her bedtime.
O Jenny and Tia are Sara's friends.
These words tell us to think what the story is mostly about.
Q James

Figure 9.3. The words *main idea* catch James's and Quinten's attention. They know they need to ignore minor details and determine what was most important in the story.

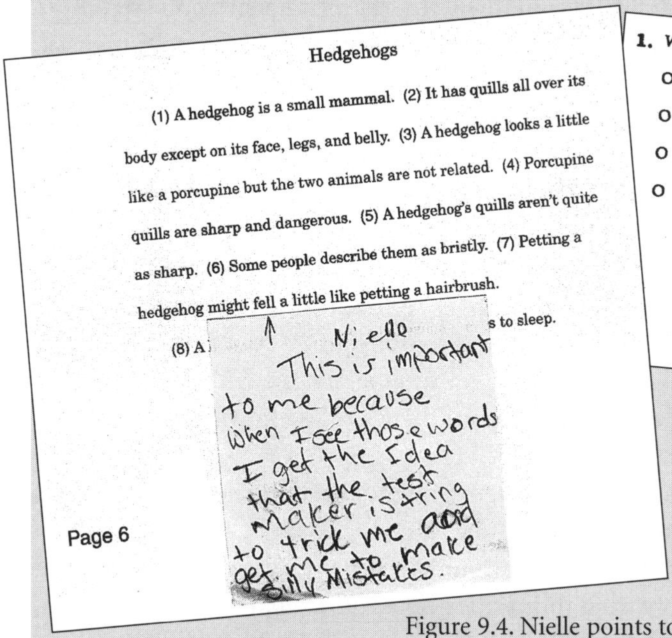
Hedgehogs
(1) A hedgehog is a small mammal. (2) It has quills all over its body except on its face, legs, and belly. (3) A hedgehog looks a little like a porcupine but the two animals are not related. (4) Porcupine quills are sharp and dangerous. (5) A hedgehog's quills aren't quite as sharp. (6) Some people describe them as bristly. (7) Petting a hedgehog might fell a little like petting a hairbrush.
(8) A
s to sleep.
Nielle
This is important to me because when I see those words I get the Idea that the test maker is tring to trick me and get me to make silly Mistakes.
Page 6

Figure 9.4. Nielle points to a specific word in the passage that is important to her process as she works through an editing task.

STORIES FROM THE CLASSROOM

Discovering How to Think Like a Test Taker . . . Determining What's Important

By Missy Matthews

The fifth-grade students in rooms 34 and 35 were in the midst of studying how to determine importance. Every morning during reading and writing workshop, Veronica had been helping students recognize when, why, and how they knew something was important in text. Next door with Rachel, they talked each afternoon about the ways mathematicians and researchers determine importance in their work. It was an impressive instructional dance between the two classrooms. Even though Veronica teaches reading and writing and Rachel teaches mathematics, science, and social studies, they both used one common thinking strategy to connect the learning across the day and between the two classrooms.

The students in rooms 34 and 35 were the kind of students we read about in other testing books and articles; the kind to whom standardized tests were a mystery. Far too often they brought little background knowledge about test passages with them on testing day. The life experiences and language of these students were different from the knowledge test makers assume all students bring with them to school. Rachel and Veronica's students exemplified the concerns many people raise about the racial, cultural, and socioeconomic bias inherent in any standardized test.

For the students in rooms 34 and 35, comments like "They're just trying to confuse me" or "The questions are always tricky" were all too common when talking about high-stakes tests.

Veronica and Rachel desperately wanted their students' learning, the huge cognitive leaps they saw every day in their classrooms, to be evident to others, including the people who value the results of state tests. But if the students in rooms 34 and 35 were going to demonstrate what they knew on test day, they would have to understand the tricks of the trade: how proficient test takers think about their work. And that's where I got to help.

With a two-part reading test item in hand, the students and I gathered around the overhead projector.

"I can see by the charts around your room that you've had many conversations about how readers and writers determine what's most important. Today, I have another type of reading for us to consider. It's actually a reading test, something very similar to CSAP." I put a copy of "London Eye Sees First Passengers," a released item from the Texas Department of Education's website, on the overhead.

"Take a few minutes to look this over. As you skim through the pages, I want you to decide what you think is most important."

Even though this was unfamiliar work, I didn't want to launch our conversation by demonstrating my own processes. First, I wanted to hear their initial thinking, their insights.

I watched as students worked. Veronica had taught them that whenever possible, they should write their thinking on the text because "thinking not captured is often thinking lost." As I scanned the room, a handful of students wrote feverishly. Most students had a thought or two jotted in the margins. Another handful flipped, flipped, and flipped the test pages searching for something, anything, they could say they noticed.

"What do you think is important?" I asked.

"Titles are most important," Alfonso said.

"It looks like a newspaper, so it's probably a reporter talking," Rustin added.

"I think it's going to be about London," Alex said.

"Why is that important, Alex?" I probed.

"It's in the title, so it's important."

"So you're thinking along the lines of Alfonso . . . that titles are important," I said.

Pointing to a caption under a picture on the first page, Anthony added, "Knowing this helps you know what you'll be reading about."

"Does that help set your purpose as a reader?" I asked.

"Yeah, I guess," Anthony responded.

"Having a purpose is important to me as a reader also, Anthony. Thanks for adding this thought." I had been hoping one of the students would bring up the idea of purpose someplace in this first look at tests.

"On page four, it's a letter. It's different from the article," Vivianna said, bringing our attention back to the test sample.

Relying on her background knowledge about why anyone would write a letter, Reyna added, "I think someone is trying to persuade someone."

Connecting these two thoughts, Rustin said, "London is in the letter also. Something must happen in London and the letter must sort of repeat what the article says. I'm just predicting."

Since many of the ideas shared were actually inferences rather than thoughts about what was most important, I decided it made sense at this point to model my own thinking.

"I think it's important that there are two different pieces of text. Test makers often do this and ask the test taker to compare the two pieces. That will be important for me to remember as I read."

"I go to the questions and answers first because I think they're most important," Abby said. "When I see them, I know what I'm looking for in the story. I have a purpose."

With voices and insights beginning to fill the room, I decided it was time to get students to go deeper.

"Since we have some good initial thinking, I want you to find a partner to continue this conversation. Work with one other person and really get into the test. Look for what's important to you as a test taker. Go ahead and mark up the test, because when we come back together, I'll want you to share specific examples to support your deeper, more sophisticated thinking."

Students headed off to the tables positioned just outside the whole-group gathering area. A few students were curiously quiet during the craft lesson, so I looked around to see where they had ended up. They were the first students I conferred with once everyone had settled in for composing time. I knew that these short check-in conferences were all they would need to get going.

After helping those three pairs, Veronica and I decided to take Yetta Goodman's sage advice and spend a few minutes "kid-watching." Standing back to observe let us see what was really going on in the classroom.

Looking across a handful of papers, I noticed that students were struggling to decide what was important. Nearly everything was underlined, indicating that the students believed nearly everything was essential.

I also noticed that comments scripted in the margins were personal. Students were writing, "Wow, that's a long way!" or "That's tight!" They were reacting to the text as if they were reading the local newspaper. These students knew how to respond to their reading; they'd done it all year. But successful test takers don't generally respond this way. Because Veronica's students didn't know the expectations of testing and didn't know the ways this genre differed from their daily reading, they didn't know how to think like proficient test takers.

Cierra turned the rain stick over as a signal to gather back in the large group. Students formed a circle on the carpet as I turned the overhead back on, again projecting the test's first page up on the classroom screen.

"What did you notice is most important as test takers?" I took out my green transparency pen to record the second round of insights.

"I think the first sentence is important, because it tells me what the London Eye is. That was confusing to me in the title, but the first sentence tells me it's a Ferris wheel," Kimberly began.

Cierra added, "The second paragraph tells us how it was built."

"It says it can carry twenty-five passengers. That's a lot!" Orlando said.

"In the last paragraph, the word *reaction* is underlined. Maybe they'll ask a question about it. Like a question about what it means," Josue said.

"Josue, I think you've figured out something about tests. An underlined word is often a signal the test maker uses to let us know there might be a question about that word. As a matter of fact, did anyone get to question number two? That's exactly the question you were expecting, Josue, when you noticed that underlined word. Let's look through the possible answers to see which is correct."

After we agreed that choice F was the right answer, I said, "Let's see if we can synthesize our thinking into a few bullets. How do we determine what's important on a test? What big ideas have we figured out as a result of our work today?"

We took a few minutes to capture our thinking. The list was short, but it was a start.

How do we determine what's important on a test?
- By reading the questions first
  —Abby
- By going back to the text to find evidence
  —Cierra
- By looking for underlined or bold words
  —Josue

Veronica and I debriefed the lesson over lunch. From the way her students had reacted to this first experience using released test items as part of their reading and writing workshop, a map for future lessons began to emerge:

- Students needed to become much more familiar with the way tests are set up—they needed to have additional experience with a variety of samples.
- Students needed to know that test evaluators aren't typically looking for personal responses from test takers.
- In terms of their study of determining importance, students needed to observe the ways proficient test takers think their way through a test.

Veronica decided her next craft lesson would start with a think-aloud, one in which she'd model the ways her internal dialogue about determining importance changed when she took a test. She was thankful she'd planned on spending another few weeks with determining what's important as her instructional focus.

Revisiting Determining What's Important—Test Taking as Writers

By Patrick A. Allen

As I sat on the park bench in the gathering area of my classroom, I looked at the students gathered around my feet. They were former students I had invited in to talk about writing as test takers. All of them had had previous strategy instruction, and our goal was to revisit determining what's important as writers, as test takers. I explained that I was going to be teaching determining what's important to my current group of third graders and needed their help in planning. I wanted to see what they remembered about this strategy. The specifics they recalled would help me know what had stayed with them, what had made the biggest impression. I also wanted their help extending this study to include test taking.

To guide our craft lesson for the morning, I started the conversation with a simple focus question, something I think carefully about as I plan. On the chart paper I wrote, "How do wise test takers determine what's most important when writing?" I asked the students to dwell on this question for a minute or two. After giving them a few minutes, I began, "What are you thinking?"

I charted their answers to this initial question (see Figure 9.5).

As they were sharing, I noticed how many different strategies were coming into play as they thought about determining what's important as writers. I asked them to take a moment to look over the chart to see what

Figure 9.5

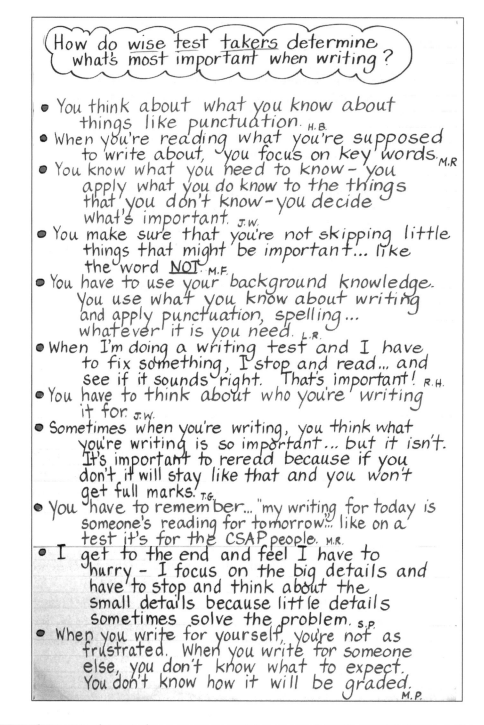

they noticed. Were there any patterns? I was struck by the sophistication of their comments. But one thing seemed to stick out—the idea of how a standardized writing test is *graded*. These students had all taken a CSAP writing test and seemed curious about how it was scored. I decided to talk to them about this important issue.

Based on Mason's comment ("When you write for someone else, you don't know what to expect. You don't know how it will be graded."), I asked, "Would it be important for you to know how it's going to be graded? Actually, we say 'scored' when we're talking about a standardized test." I was intrigued by his focus on grading and how it fit into the strategy of determining importance. I thought it was worthy of a few moments to veer away from my plan.

"You'd be more careful and say, 'Oh they're going to want me to do this right,' and you'd be more willing to fix it," Luke said.

Chauncey added, "Maybe if you knew how they would grade it, you'd improve on what you did last year. You'd know what to go back and check. You'd improve your writing to what they need to know."

Madison popped into the conversation. "You have to think and say, 'Okay, this is going to have to be understandable, am I doing this right? Can I make it look better?' If you knew what they were looking for, you'd focus on those parts."

"You're exactly right, Madison," I said. "It's about knowing your audience and changing your writing to fit both the audience and the purpose. If you could decide what is most important, that would probably make you score a bit higher."

Justin added, "If we knew what they were looking for, we could focus on those things and the ones we think are important. We could ask ourselves, 'Will they understand this? Does this make sense?'"

"So you're telling me that it's helpful if your teachers share some writing samples with you. Would it be helpful to hear about the CSAP expectations and maybe see the rubric they use to grade your work?" I asked.

Heads nodded in agreement. "But not too much," someone said. "Sometimes teachers spend way too much time talking about testing. We need to know, but they go on and on and on." I nodded in response.

Hannah said, "If we knew what to work on throughout the year, we'd be absolutely sure of what's important for you to know to do well."

"I remember I hated CSAP samples, I hated them," Justin said. "But after I saw them, I felt like I did better because going into it I knew my stuff. That helped me see the similarities between the two—my own writing and CSAP writing."

"You guys are so wise," I said. "I can't wait to share that thinking with my friends and colleagues. If you come up with any other ideas, let me know. I'd love to hear your ideas and suggestions. I didn't realize how important it was to share the scoring samples with you. I will definitely do that with my third graders. Thanks for your help. Mason, thanks for bringing that issue up for us to discuss.

"Here's something that might look familiar to you." I placed a sample writing prompt on the document camera (see Figure 9.6). "It's one page of a

> **Write a paragraph in which you describe something you like to do and explain <u>why</u> you enjoy it.**
>
> **You <u>may</u> use the space below to plan your writing.**
>
> **Begin your paragraph here. You do not have to use all the lines. Just write on as many as you need.**

Figure 9.6

third-grade writing practice test. Let's say this was the writing you were being asked to do. What's important? Today, I'd like to spend a few minutes looking it over and talking about what you think is important as a test taker."

The room was again abuzz with voices.

Chase began, "First of all, you should always read the directions before you do anything. That's important."

Parker said, "The word *paragraph* tells me that I won't be writing just a sentence. I can't just tell what the thing is I like to do; I have to write a whole paragraph about it."

"You're right, Parker. Even though we don't usually write single paragraphs, we do in this case. You know that writers learn to paragraph only to make it easier for their readers. But this is an example of how writing for tests is different from the writing we normally do," I said.

"The word *why* tells me to explain my thinking and the word *may* tells me it's not necessary," Mackenzie mentioned. She was very focused on important words.

"And the word *describe* is really important," Taylor added. "Once a teacher told me that there are describing words and telling words, so you need to choose the words you use to describe something carefully."

"Good point, Taylor. It's important that we choose the best words to convey our meaning and that meet the requirements of what they are asking us to write. That's an important key to writing for tests."

Chauncey noticed the amount of space provided for planning and writing. He said, "When I see that much space, well . . . I think you have to be more thoughtful, so only important things come out. Knowing about space gets the best parts out of you . . . It puts out better words that show you're a smart writer."

"I always worry about space, Chauncey," I said. "I like how you said 'gets the best parts out of you.' That's important to remember as a test taker. What a great way to say it. As writers, getting those best parts should always be a goal."

Sydney smiled and said, "I see that word *plan* and it means I have to jot down my ideas. As I make a web or list, I have to think, 'Why is this important?' It keeps you prepared to write."

"I'm still thinking about that word *paragraph* in the prompt," I said. "Can we talk about that for a few minutes? I know you all know how to use paragraphs to alert your reader about a break in a piece, but when you're asked to write just one, what goes through your mind? When it's for someone else, what is important?" Again, I charted their thinking (see Figure 9.7).

"You guys did some great work today. I can tell you're thinking a lot about the idea of determining importance as test takers. Before we go, let's think about our original question, 'How do wise test takers determine what's most important when writing?' What are you thinking now?"

Mackenzie said, "You don't know who you're writing for, so it has to be the best it can be."

Madison added, "You should look for important details in the directions."

"Make your writing descriptive. Make sure it has important words," Olivia said.

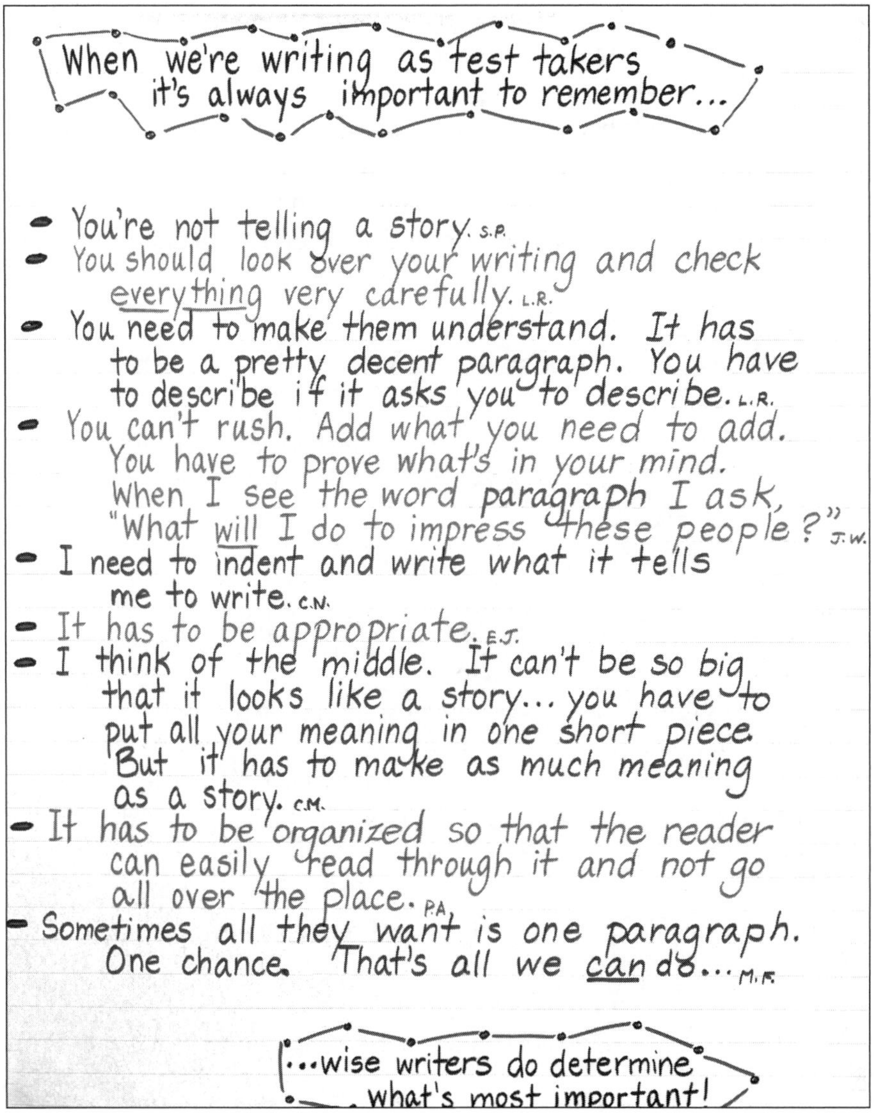

Figure 9.7

When we're writing as test takers it's always important to remember...

- You're not telling a story. s.p.
- You should look over your writing and check <u>everything</u> very carefully. L.R.
- You need to make them understand. It has to be a pretty decent paragraph. You have to describe if it asks you to describe. L.R.
- You can't rush. Add what you need to add. You have to prove what's in your mind. When I see the word paragraph I ask, "What <u>will</u> I do to impress these people?" J.W.
- I need to indent and write what it tells me to write. c.N.
- It has to be appropriate. E.J.
- I think of the middle. It can't be so big that it looks like a story... you have to put all your meaning in one short piece. But it has to make as much meaning as a story. c.M.
- It has to be organized so that the reader can easily read through it and not go all over the place. P.A.
- Sometimes all they want is one paragraph. One chance. That's all we <u>can</u> do... M.F.

...wise writers do determine what's most important!

Taylor said, "Sometimes you have to use more detail so you don't forget anything."

"If I'm answering questions on the writing test, I should always determine the best answer. I need to put thought into it," Chase added. I jotted down a reminder to myself to remember that issue; we would also have to talk about some actual writing-test questions.

Parker said, "You can't just guess. You have to think. You have to look carefully at everything."

"You have to be able to think about what you're writing or doing so other people can understand what you're doing. That's what's important," Emma added.

"You're all right. We have to think carefully about this idea of determining importance as writers. I can't wait to share your thinking with my kids. I also want you to tuck this thinking into your heads so you can use it when you're taking a test. You're so wise and smart. Thanks for letting me pick your brains today."

As I sent the kids back to their classrooms, I couldn't wait to reread my notes. I knew their thinking would be useful during our upcoming study of determining what's most important. I also planned to share all their insights with their teachers, because I knew they'd want to incorporate testing into their instruction.

POSSIBILITIES: Craft Lessons for Determining What Is Important

What test words and phrases tell us we're supposed to determine importance?
List test-specific language prompts a test taker uses to sift through test material for necessary important content. (E.g., questions that include phrases such as *main idea, mainly about, summarize, essential.*)

What essential content-related words from the test should we include in our answers?
Practice scanning test materials looking for specific vocabulary necessary for adding precision to written answers. (E.g., "I need to compose a short, constructed response explaining how I extended a stamp design. The question includes words like *rotation*, *90 degrees*, and *elements*. Those are the specific terms I should use in my writing, too.")

How does reading the questions first help us know what to pay attention to as we determine what's most important?
Demonstrate ways previewing questions creates a mental filter for the test taker. (E.g., "It looks like there are four questions about the 'Great

Discoveries in Science' time line. That must be a pretty important part of this test section. I'll read it with extra care.")

How does the format of the test item help us determine what's most important?
Link specific test formatting with determining importance. (E.g., "When there are two parts to a math question, the second step is usually printed in bold. That's our reminder not to forget an important part.")

How would determining importance help us make sense of this material if we found it outside of a testing situation?
Compare ways determining importance supports meaning making in various contents and contexts. (E.g., "In any other situation, deciding what's most important would be directly linked to my questions and my purpose. But in a testing situation, what's essential to me doesn't matter as much.")

Chapter 10
TEST TAKERS

Monitor for Meaning and Problem-Solve When Meaning Breaks Down

From their training regimen to their diets to their highly individualized windup and release, great pitchers continually monitor their ability. They check to see if what they're doing is leading them to lower earned run averages and winning records. Speed guns, video analysis, pitch counts, and win/loss ratios provide explicit information, helping pitchers decide whether they're getting it ("I'm really on today!") or not ("I'm getting pounded!").

Taking a test can sometimes feel like the seventh game of the World Series—there can be a great deal at stake. Pitchers understand this pressure. But how do test takers monitor whether or not they're making sense in the middle of a test, when, unlike a pitcher, they can't call time and have a quick conference on the mound with their pitching coach and catcher?

Test takers . . .

- use test directions to help set a purpose for their work—and return to these directions to clarify expectations when they're confused. ("I think in this section I'm supposed to figure out what the data on these line graphs mean, but I'm not sure how I'm supposed to show my work. Oh yeah, the directions told me to extend the graph fifteen years.")
- monitor their ongoing understanding as they move from item to item, section to section, rather than waiting until they're finished with a test. ("Okay, I think this first couple of poems are talking about . . . so now I can keep going. Stopping every now and then really helps me feel like I'm making sense of this test even before I get to the questions at the end.")
- discriminate between passage understanding and item understanding. ("I get that this whole article explains how the water cycle is influenced by heat, wind patterns, and elevation. But I'm not quite sure what this specific question about evaporation is asking. I better reread the question.")

- keep audience (i.e., the evaluators) and purpose (i.e., showing what they know to get a good score) in mind throughout the test-taking process. ("These guys don't know me, so I really have to show that I understand poetry. I think I did a good job of naming how this poet used a darkened room to describe loneliness.")

Student Examples—Naming What They Notice About Tests and Monitoring for Meaning and Problem-Solving

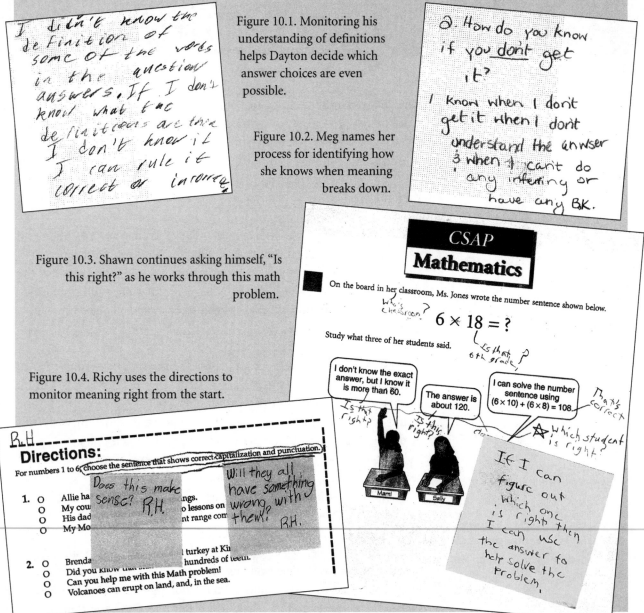

Figure 10.1. Monitoring his understanding of definitions helps Dayton decide which answer choices are even possible.

Figure 10.2. Meg names her process for identifying how she knows when meaning breaks down.

Figure 10.3. Shawn continues asking himself, "Is this right?" as he works through this math problem.

Figure 10.4. Richy uses the directions to monitor meaning right from the start.

Opera or the Broncos . . . Monitoring as Writers

By Cheryl Zimmerman

A remake of the song "Route 66" signaled twenty-three third-grade writers to gather on the rug in our classroom meeting area. Paul pushed the CD player's power button after the last of the lyrics played.

"Today we're going to think about being metacognitive and how we monitor for understanding. First, I want you to remember the assembly we attended last week. You know, the opera performance?" I scanned the room. "Nancy, what do you remember?"

"They had fancy costumes and there was a castle in the background. There was lots of singing and we were allowed to yell *bravo* only when it was over."

"I remember that, too," I said. "And I remember that during the performance, we sat flat on the floor, trying not to move around much or make any noise that might distract the performers or the other audience members. Now, I want you to think about another special day at school—the day we got to participate in the Bronco Training Camp Obstacle Course. Remember that day?"

Armon's hand flew into the air. "I loved that day! We ran around outside catching footballs, zigzagging through cones, and blasting into pretend blockers."

"Was it okay to yell and scream, Armon?"

"Yeah. After we listened to the directions at each station, we could make all the noise we wanted. We cheered on the sidelines and we jumped around even when it wasn't our turn."

"Why were the expectations different at the opera assembly?" I asked.

"They're two different kinds of things," said Marc. "Running around was okay at one, but not at the other. What's *appropriate* changes, depending on what kind of thing it is."

"How do you think that connects to being metacognitive?" After a second or two, Ruyee raised his hand.

"When you're metacognitive, you're aware of where you are and what you're supposed to be doing. You think about what's okay and what isn't okay. You know what you understand and what you don't understand. At the opera, we needed to sit pretty still, and it wasn't okay to be noisy. At the Bronco thing, it was okay to run around and yell."

"You are one metacognitive guy, Ruyee. Now let's switch gears a bit and think about being metacognitive as writers. If you're writing in your writer's notebook, what kinds of things are okay? Maggie?"

"It's okay to just play around with your ideas. If your handwriting is a little sloppy, it's okay as long as you can read it. It's okay to leave something unfinished. It's okay to draw something that might help you with your piece."

"Thanks, Maggie. What else, you guys?"

"It's okay to let your imagination go a little wild, and you don't have to worry about perfect spelling," said Blake.

"All right, now take a look at this." I projected a test writing prompt for the group to see. "How is this kind of writing different from writing in your writer's notebook?"

"It's way different," Scott answered. "There are directions to follow, so letting your imagination go wild probably won't work. This prompt is about a favorite holiday, and it says you have to write a paragraph, so you can't really play around with a poem or a list like you might in your notebook."

"Plus, there's only so much space to use," Andrea said, shaking her head. "You have to understand that you can't keep turning the page like you can in your notebook. It's weird, but it's the way it is on a writing test."

"What about your handwriting and your spelling?" I asked.

"Someone else has to be able to read it pretty easily," said Trisha. "You need to spell correctly—or at least reasonably. And your handwriting needs to be legible. You won't be able to tell the test grader that you meant for that sloppy letter to be a *u*, not an *a*."

"It's like the opera assembly and the Bronco thing," Hannah said. "The way you behave depends on where you are and what you're supposed to do. The way you write depends on what you're doing as a writer, and on who might be reading your writing."

"You're sharing some great thinking about being metacognitive as writers," I said. "As you go off to work today, I want you to spend a few minutes jotting some thoughts on this Venn diagram. Compare and contrast writing in a writer's notebook with responding to a prompt on a writing test. Bring your Venn diagram to our reflecting time at the end of our workshop and be prepared to teach us."

Over the course of the workshop, third-grade writers filled Venn diagrams with similarities and differences, heightening their awareness of the unique demands test writing presents. And, in a broader sense, heightening the awareness that throughout their lives different experiences present different expectations (see Figure 10.5 for one example).

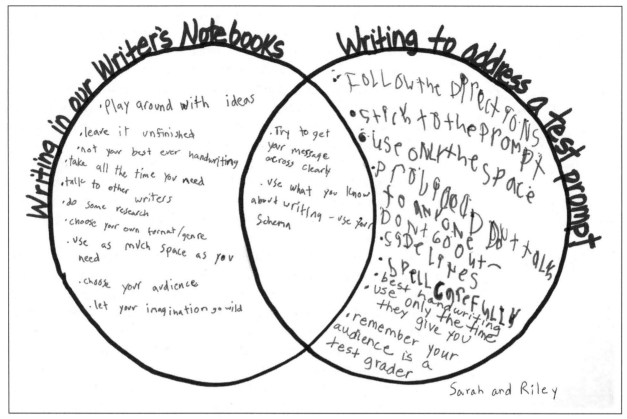

Figure 10.5

Seventh Graders Name When They Get It and When They Don't

By Missy Matthews

Conversations, joking, and typical hallway teasing lingered as the bell rang. Entering their classroom, Liz Swanson's seventh-grade scientists found their seats around the black lab tables.

"Hey, guys! How are you today?"

After hearing several stories from students about their day, the previous night's basketball win, and their favorite video games, I began to explain our work.

"I've got a question for you. When you're working on an experiment or reading a chapter in your science book, how do you know you're on track with the work? How do you know you get it? Turn to your table partners and talk for just a couple of minutes."

After a few minutes of quiet buzz, I called everyone back. "What have you come up with? Luis?"

"Because I have background knowledge. It's something we have already studied in class so the new work is easy."

"I know I'm getting it because I don't have to guess at it," Michael added.

"I know I'm understanding something because it feels like I'm getting all the right answers to the questions at the end of the chapter or that I could tell somebody else what the chapter was about," Paulina said.

"Thanks. That's a great start," I said. "I knew you'd have a lot to say about making sense as scientists. Today, I want to take another step with this conversation. I want to think about how we know we're making sense, what I'll call 'monitoring understandings,' when we take a standardized science test."

At the mention of tests, a shared groan rippled across the classroom. From their body language, the rolled eyes, and the tilting back in chairs, I knew I'd hit a sour note. As seventh graders, they'd just about had their fill of standardized tests. They'd become all too familiar with the yearly routine: they spend hours every spring taking the state test, and they receive feedback in the form of a letter home months later listing scores that mean virtually nothing to them or their parents.

"I know . . . This is a tough topic for all of us," I said. "That's why I'm so interested in this question about monitoring. I want to see if using a strategy you already know so well in your typical science work can help you feel more powerful, more able, when you find yourself in a situation that's really uncomfortable. Are you game?"

The kids nodded . . . not enthusiastically, but they nodded.

Strategy instruction was nothing new to these students. As middle schoolers, they had studied this work across content-area classes for the previous two years. Since this was their first time to consider their thinking as test takers, I decided to start with a think-aloud.

"I have a page from a science test I found on the Internet. I thought it would be a good example for us to explore. Let me share my thinking as a test taker with you. As I think aloud, watch me and pay close attention to what I'm saying. When I'm finished, I'll ask you to share some of the things you noticed." I put the sample on the overhead projector.

"The first question says, 'Which of the following is the product of a chemical change?' I'm thinking about this word *product*. It means result. I can't name any chemical changes, but let's see if I can eliminate a couple of choices.

"Ice isn't the product of a chemical change. I think rust is, but before I choose rust, I'm going to read through the other choices to make sure I can eliminate them. Sawdust wouldn't be a chemical change. Saltwater isn't one either. So it has to be choice B, rust."

"Do you mean process of elimination?" Corey blurted out. "Is that the same thing as monitoring?"

"Exactly. That's one way I know I'm understanding. When I know enough to eliminate choices, or when I feel like I don't know enough about a test question to do any eliminating, I'm paying attention to whether I'm making sense. Corey, thanks for naming it for us. Let's keep going.

"With number sixteen, there's a chart listing three days of weather forecast. The question sitting below the chart asks what Saturday's forecast will *most likely* be. First of all, *most likely* means I'll need to make an inference. To make a smart inference, I better look for a pattern. Knowing that I should look for a pattern is a way I monitor my understanding as I take a test.

"According to the chart, each day the temperature gets warmer and the chance of rain decreases. I can anticipate this pattern will continue, but I don't have a lot of data. Choice C is the only choice where the temperature increases and the chance of rain decreases. That makes sense."

The next section of the test began with a paragraph describing how a boy answers his own questions about cooking pasta in boiling water by conducting an experiment. The paragraph was followed by a results chart and three questions. I read the paragraph aloud to the students and again shared my thinking.

"I don't get what this paragraph is talking about. Maybe I should read the graph and the question to see if that helps me figure out what the paragraph is talking about. The question says, 'Based on his experiment, Antoine thinks that adding sugar to water would produce the same results as the salt. This idea is best referred to as _____?'

"Oh, now I get it. I don't even have to understand the paragraph. What Antoine's doing is called a hypothesis, choice A. I know that because I know that scientists make hypotheses."

I moved away from the overhead and asked the students to tell me what they had seen and heard.

Luis said, "You were checking to make sure you understood each question."

"Right . . . but what did I do to show you that I was checking to make sure I was understanding?"

"You kept going. You tried to find the right answer," he clarified.

"Oh, so I was persistent, is that what you mean? When I know something isn't quite right, and it's important, I can stick with it as long as I have to. What else did you notice?" I probed.

"You were using the information they gave you on the second question to help you figure out the answer to the third question. That's how you knew you got it. You knew you could use the information for other questions," Ty answered.

"And you looked for patterns," added Mike.

"As a test taker, that pattern helped me eliminate incorrect answers," I said. "Looking for patterns is a way I can be monitoring my meaning making."

Mallory said, "On the last one, you focused on the question when you didn't understand the paragraph before it."

"You're right. Having that question in my head gave me something to do when I was confused. The question helped me not quit when the test made no sense. Okay, it's your turn. You've watched me have a go with one example. Here's another practice test. Remember, right now it's not about finishing the test. Really pay attention to the questions you understand. Be ready to tell us how you know those test parts made sense. And, just as important, keep track of the things that are confusing. Sharing those insights will be critical. Record all your thinking in the margins of the test. I'll be around to talk with several of you."

Students got busy. Most chose to work with partners or in triads. Notebook in hand, I began to confer.

I had noticed Zane was very quiet during my think-aloud, and yet he began to work diligently on his own. I was curious about his process.

"Hey, Zane, how's it going?"

"Good." I should have expected that one.

"I notice you've already answered most of the questions. Is this test easy for you?"

"Yes."

"What are you thinking about this idea of monitoring for meaning?"

"I don't think I really need to do any of that. I remember all this stuff from our health unit. I already have background knowledge. Like with this one, I imagined the little gear moving a full turn and the big gear could move only a partial turn," he said as he pointed to one of the questions.

"Okay, that's what I want you to pay attention to. How do you know that your answers are right, that the questions make sense? See if you notice yourself doing anything other than using your schema." I headed to another table.

I pulled up next to Myke. "Hey, Myke, what are you working on?"

"I'm doing number two."

"Does it make sense to you? How do you know?"

"I know *classify* means to describe and name."

"How does that help you?"

"I know what to do since I know that word. We've studied it," he said.

"So you know what you're being asked. How does that help you figure out the correct answer?"

"It just hit me. The others don't make sense."

There was a lot I could talk about with Myke, but the class was becoming restless. Their stamina for this sort of work wasn't what it needed to be for me to continue, so I invited everyone to find a good place to stop while I jotted a few things I wanted to think more about:

- How can I help students name their thinking in more articulate, usable ways?
- How can I help students build the kind of stamina necessary to get through tasks that aren't particularly engaging?
- How can I help students not quit just because the task is hard or because it's something they don't value?

Once everyone focused back in with me, I asked each of them to write down how she had tried to put today's lesson to use. I knew Liz and I would be able to use these responses for future planning.

POSSIBILITIES: Craft Lessons for Monitoring Meaning and Problem-Solving

Because tests sometimes change midway through, what things do we need to pay attention to so we're sure we stay on the right track?

Notice when test directions, test format, and test expectations change. (E.g., "In the first set of multiple-choice answers I had to choose a synonym for each underlined word, but now the directions say to choose an opposite. Wow, that's confusing. I'm glad I read the second set of directions.")

How can we take what we know about the way writers revise to help us make sure our test answers make sense?

Extend the definition and concept of revision. (E.g., "The question's telling me to explain whether or not my scatter plot shows a positive or negative relationship between x and y. I better reread what I wrote to make sure I used the word *positive*, and I better add the labels x and y.")

How do we use the process of elimination with tests?

Notice how to eliminate unnecessary and unreasonable answers. (E.g., "Choice B uses the word *never*. I know in science, 'never' doesn't happen. I need to read the other choices for words like that.")

What are the ways we maintain the stamina necessary to get to the end of the test?

Recognize the internal motivators and external restraints of test taking. (E.g., "I have five more pages and I really want to finish, so I better keep an eye on the clock" or "There's a stop sign on page seven. I can't go past that.")

How would my monitoring and problem-solving be different when I'm taking a test?

Chart similarities and differences between test-based metacognition and typical school metacognition. (E.g., "When I'm writing in my journal, I know I can write about anything, but on the test, topic choice is determined for me. There's no wiggle room. I need to be precise.")

Still Learning About Tests

*I've come to believe there are only two things
you need in any new teaching situation to
succeed—humility and inquiry.*
LISA DELPIT

◆

T hrough our inquiry, we've learned a lot. We've learned . . .

• that tests really can become a useful context for exploring thinking;
• that the thinking strategies we've come to know so well in reading,
  writing, research, and math are useful tools for understanding standardized tests;
• that our students are indeed our best teachers.

Yes, we've learned a lot. As Ron Ritchhart (2002) reminds us, learning is
always a product of thinking. And, this book represents our current best
thinking. But we also know we've still got so much more to learn.

Our final two chapters share a few lingering questions and the one thing
we know for sure—that if we remain true to what we believe, true to our
sense of professional integrity, we're on the right path.

Chapter 11 Q & A—Weaving Thinking Together with Testing

The moment we have answers, there is no dialogue. Questions unite people. Answers divide them.

ELIE WIESEL

◆

No matter how hard we've tried to paint an honest, useful portrait of our journey toward making thoughtful decisions about standardized tests, we know we've undoubtedly left some of our readers wanting more. There is still so much for all of us to learn!

Here are a few questions we've been asked, and have indeed asked ourselves, as this book unfolded. We hope these ending thoughts offer insights. But more important, we hope they offer a challenge for asking the questions we've not yet even thought of . . . eventually leading you to help all students *put thinking to the test*.

If I do all the things described in this book, will my students' scores really go up?

Unlike the latest fitness fad equipment, this book doesn't come with a money-back guarantee. We've never proclaimed that approaching standardized tests from a thinking stance is a silver bullet. That wasn't our goal. There is no guarantee that scores will rise; otherwise we would have named this book *Practice, Practice, Practice* or *Just Do It . . . and Watch Your Scores Go Up.*

For the most part, students in our classrooms are consistently proficient test takers. Our colleagues have reported that their students' scores have remained consistent and some have indeed shown improvement. Many researchers, including Trabasso and Bouchard (2002), Newmann, Bryke, and Nagaoka (2001), and Block, Gambrell, and Pressley (2002), have documented the many ways that learning in a thinking-centered classroom leads students to improved scores on standardized measures. But because every group of students is different, nothing is a "gimme." There are times when the scores come back and a sense of disappointment and puzzlement prevails.

The good news is that even in those disappointing moments, all is not lost. We believe that if we tap into our students' metacognition, they can't help but grow as thinkers. And that has to make a positive difference in their daily learning—even the learning measured by standardized tests. We can sleep well at night knowing that a thinking strategy approach benefits students, both for and beyond the scope of "the test."

It seems like I could be "doing tests" all year. How does the use of released test items fit into an already full curriculum?

Our plates are too full, aren't they? It really isn't about doing tests. Instead, it's about using test items as a regular source for shared work. We strive to incorporate the thinking standardized tests demand into our ongoing instruction. By using test materials in craft lessons across the year, students come to understand that tests aren't something to be feared, ignored, or taken lightly.

We are not advocates of everyday drill and kill with test practice. Every day, no. Periodically, and thoughtfully, purposefully, yes. On average, we use released items a couple of times a month. There are times that test items seem to fit. For example, when we're studying poetry, why not study the ways test makers test a reader's knowledge of poetry? We also see the benefits of studying tests as a unique genre. Just as we might study essays intensely for a couple of weeks, we study the unique features of tests in the same manner.

When we plan for a study of inferring or determining importance, we include the ways the strategy works with fiction, nonfiction, poetry, content materials, *and* test samples.

Much of this book revolves around teaching reading comprehension/thinking strategies. Is there a "right order" I should use when planning my year?

We firmly believe there is no hierarchy or prescription when it comes to teaching and learning thinking strategies. As is true with so many other curricular goals, the "right order" depends heavily on the unique group of students in our care. Some years we've started with asking questions, and other years it's synthesis, or determining importance. It might make sense to begin the year with a strategy we feel particularly comfortable with, knowing all the while that our students will stretch our thinking to new heights. What we do know is that all the strategies should be taught explicitly. We need to take the time for students to gradually gain a sense of independence and responsibility for each one. Strategic thinking should not be relegated to what Donald Graves has called the "cha-cha-cha curriculum." Depth is better than breadth—regardless of the order.

What's the easiest way to get my hands on various released test items? Do I need to purchase test practice booklets?

Released test items are available on district and state education department websites. When we were looking for samples to use with our own students, we discovered that many items were similar from state to state. Published test preparation booklets are also widely available.

Finding the test samples is the easy part.

Deciding how to incorporate these items into our day-to-day instruction is what takes thought, collaboration, and a purpose beyond simply practicing tests. Our caution would be to choose wisely.

If my school or school district still believes in spending six weeks on "test prep," how can I make a case for helping my students not just practice test items, but really explore the thinking standardized tests demand?

There is much to be said about the power of student engagement. We've found that approaching test practice in a thoughtful, thought-filled manner leads to increased student engagement. That might be enough of a hook to move your colleagues forward.

If not, perhaps you could conduct an informal teacher research project. Invite fellow teachers or administrators to observe and compare traditional test-prep lessons with thinking-based lessons. Interview students to gain their perspective on which approach makes them feel most prepared and efficacious. You might also participate in the committees and cohorts that make instructional decisions for your school or school district.

It isn't simply about bucking testing mandates or closing our doors to unreasonable test-preparation schedules. It's about facing these demands with integrity. It's about becoming better informed. It's about never losing track of our students.

How might I share this new vision for classroom work with my students and their parents—especially if they come to me already feeling beaten down by standardized testing?

The "you've got to see it to believe it" adage really applies here. Plan a parent education evening. Spend an hour in a workshop complete with a craft lesson, a composing session where students and their parents think through test items together, and a reflecting session encouraging everyone to share new insights and questions. End the evening by reiterating the many ways classroom time can be used to enhance understanding rather than simply practicing filling in blanks and darkening bubbles.

Like their parents, students need to understand the roles tests play in our classrooms and in their lives. Seeing the way their thinking makes tests doable gives them a sense of power, a belief in their capacity as thinkers.

Some of your vignettes include behaviors students aren't really allowed to do on tests, such as writing on test items, using sticky notes, and working with partners. If they can't do these things when they take a real test, why would we have them do these things as we work through sample test items?

Although it's true that test takers typically can't use a highlighter or benefit from their neighbor's best thinking when taking a standardized test, inviting them to practice these behaviors leads to better metacognition during the actual test. Using the strategies effortlessly and independently has always been our goal with strategy instruction. It's never just about "doing the strategy," because it doesn't really matter if you make a schema connection or create a mental image if you can't name the ways that connection or image helps you understand. This holds especially true for thinking through tests.

When students work with their peers, talking through their mental moves, they're developing a habit of focusing on thinking in all situations, even testing situations. And by jotting notes in the margin or recording insights on sticky notes to be shared later, students are making public the sort of active brain work they'll need to employ later in the privacy of actual testing sessions.

It's like any teaching framed by the gradual release of responsibility. We begin with thinking aloud, then move to shared learning and eventually to independence. It's like when gymnasts are learning to do a backflip: first we model, and then we assist them while they wear a safety harness. Eventually they can do a backflip by themselves, virtually in their sleep.

We value the instruction and the learning process, not just getting the right answer. We want students to be able to discuss the thinking behind their answers. If they can explain their thinking and share their strategies long before the day of the *big test*, they can't help but perform better when they open their testing booklet.

◆ ◆ ◆

In *Clarice Bean Spells Trouble*, author Lauren Child's main character, Clarice, desperately wants a starring role in the school production of *The Sound of Music*, and she wants to impress Mrs. Wilberton, her teacher, in the school's spelling bee. Being in nonstop trouble and having Karl, the naughtiest boy in school, as a best friend isn't helping.

But despite her quirkiness, Clarice is full of personality and spunk. The harder she works to stay out of trouble, the more trouble she tends to find. Even so, Clarice is something special. She has all the charm, uniqueness, and curiosity of the students we work with every day.

Why end our Q & A with a thumbnail sketch of *Clarice Bean Spells Trouble*? The answer is simple. It's because Clarice asks the best question of all: "Who decides what's important and what isn't?" In the case of standardized testing, someone else makes that decision, someone who sits the farthest away from the learners in our care. As we think about testing and teaching, we can all learn a little something from Clarice.

Every week, Clarice deals with the perplexities and complexities of Testing Tuesdays, where testing determines the smartness of students, with spirited curiosity. And every week, she wonders how anyone can test *real* smartness. She laments, "That's the thing about school: they might only test you for one thing, i.e., math, or spellingy type things, or punctuationy thingummybobs."

It's Clarice's belief that really important things such as how to mend a hem with a stapler, or how to draw while standing on your head, or how to get green marker out of white carpet never seem to show up on school tests measuring smartness. After all, Clarice wonders, would you rather know someone who knows how to jump out of a moving helicopter without twisting an ankle the way her hero, Ruby Redfort, can or someone who knows how to spell *grapefruit* correctly?

Like Clarice, we've come to realize that the folks who design most standardized tests can't be bothered with this kind of qualitative data.

Clarice fixates on the annoyances of the testing environment and the little details that distract her: clocks ticking away, the irritating breathing of the boy behind her, and handing in her test only to hear an "Oh deary dear" from the teacher as she collects Clarice's subpar work. Testing Tuesdays literally make Clarice nauseated. She becomes a frequent flier in the school secretary's office, hoping a phone call home will rescue her from school.

Like Clarice, our children are often faced with taking tests. Some matter, some don't matter. As we write this book, we're faced with the questions we can answer and those we can't. We're faced with Clarice's thought: "Anyway, I've been wondering, who is the person who gets to decide what's important? Because I wish it was me!"

So do we, Clarice. So do we.

Chapter 12 Integrity: It's All About Being True to Ourselves and Our Profession

We have all had those teachers, inside and outside the classroom: people who believed in us, who trusted our uniqueness, who unleashed our dormant talents, and who gave us the skills and confidence to carve away at the stone ourselves. We remember them for their gifts to us. Perhaps their greatest gift was the standard they set as curious and passionate learners.

ELLIN KEENE AND SUSAN ZIMMERMANN

◆

In a children's fable called *Belling the Cat*, a group of mice find that they can no longer go about their business because a sneaky cat constantly lurks nearby, waiting to pounce. Tired of the terror, the mice devise a clever plan. The plan involves attaching a bell to the cat's collar. The sound of the bell will provide plenty of warning of the cat's approach, allowing the mice time to find safety. Unfortunately, in the end, not one mouse volunteers to actually attach the bell to the cat's collar. The plan fails, and fear continues to rule.

Unlike the mice in the fable, teachers and school professionals have plenty of warning when it comes to the annual approach of high-stakes tests. But trepidation lingers. What if our students don't perform well? What if scores drop from last year? What if our beliefs about what is best for the students in our care don't translate to higher test scores?

Do we live in misery, compromising our beliefs to raise the scores?

Katherine Bomer, an author and nationally known literacy consultant, says no. In her article "Missing the Children: When Politics and Programs Impede Our Teaching" (2005), Bomer tells of her decision to resign from her beloved teaching position. "I told my principal that my bottom line had been crossed. I told her that a decade of fighting increased district, state, and federal intrusion into my classroom, and decreased trust in my ability and expertise as a teacher, had left me feeling like a used tube of toothpaste, squeezed and rolled up to that last, sad, thin smear on the toothbrush" (168).

Aimee Buckner, a fourth-grade teacher in Georgia and the author of the article "Teaching in a World Focused on Testing" (2002), also says no to compromising her beliefs. "Those of us with a lot of knowledge, a deep understanding of how children really learn, and a strong grasp on quality assessment need to stand strong in the face of this controversy. And that means not sacrificing our teaching, our devotion to children, or our standards of excellence for any high-stakes test" (215).

As a teacher, Cheryl has no choice but to participate, as wisely as possible, in the testing environment required by law. But as the parent of two "testing age" daughters, Cheryl decided long ago not to allow her own children to participate.

Sure, there are some easy-to-plan-and-prepare things we could put into practice in the classroom. We could copy worksheet packets designed to accompany every book read. We could require students to write to prompts three times a week. We could drill science vocabulary in lieu of spending time lost in experiments, and memorize math algorithms instead of working through rich, diverse word problems. But to what end?

Over our many years in education, the four of us have developed a strong sense of integrity. *Encarta World English Dictionary* defines integrity as "the quality of possessing and steadfastly adhering to high moral principles or professional standards" (2007). For us, the question of compromising our beliefs for high test scores is a question of integrity.

We choose to adhere to a set of professional standards best implemented in a setting where inquiry, diversity, creativity, authenticity, stamina, strategic thinking, and risk-taking are honored and encouraged. We refuse to let kids begin to believe, in Anna Quindlen's words, "that learning is a joyless succession of hoops through which they must jump, rather than a way of understanding the world" (2005, 88).

Perhaps this complex issue boils down to one question: at the end of the school day, school year, or school career, what do we want for our students? Ron Ritchhart (2002), author of the book *Intellectual Character*, puts it this way:

> *We've come to mistake curriculums, textbooks, standards, objectives, and tests as ends in themselves rather than as means to an end. Where are these standards and objectives taking us? What is the vision they are pointing toward? When all is said and done, when the last test is taken, what will stay with a student from his or her education? . . . I contend that what stays with us from our education are patterns: patterns of*

behavior, patterns of thinking, patterns of interaction. These patterns make up our character, specifically our intellectual character. Schools can do much to shape and influence these patterns. This is the kind of long-term vision we need for education: to be shapers of students' intellectual character. (8–9)

So where does that leave us? Between a rock and a hard place? Like the fabled mice, do we sit by and accept? Or do we search for ways to bring some intellectual character to the demands of high-stakes testing?

Although it is not the most perfect solution, we've created a middle ground by asking students to apply thinking strategies to the testing realm.

Of course, implementing this solution takes negotiation and hard work. Imagine a school year where "getting ready" wasn't something to do two weeks, or two months, before the test. To make this imagining real, you might have to ask yourself these questions:

- How can I plan instruction that will prepare my students for local or state testing without compromising my beliefs about learning?
- How will I investigate the thinking strategies themselves and begin to incorporate them into my teaching?
- How can I make direct links between standardized tests and the kind of testing students will encounter outside of school?
- What do I do when taking a test that my students might need to emulate?
- How do I stay focused when my stamina begins to wane?
- How do I decide what to pay attention to and what to ignore?
- How can I use all the released items and "test-prep" materials in a smart way?
- Where is my "line in the sand"? My line of integrity?

We've asked these same questions.
We've done this planning.
We've done this thinking.

In Colorado there is an annual bicycle tour called Ride the Rockies. The tour takes approximately 2,000 cyclists on a six- to seven-day ride on paved roads through Colorado's Rocky Mountains. The race is physically challenging and requires conditioning. Long before the day of the race, riders design a well-planned training regimen. The wide range of strategies required to complete the long trek determines how their regimen is structured. The training is gradual, varied, and specific—with the mental aspects of the race, the metacognitive piece, being just as crucial as the physical.

If riders begin training three weeks before the race, chances are they won't finish. If all they do is ride, ride, ride, they probably won't develop the complex capabilities necessary to compete. Isolated, disconnected trips won't help them in the long run.

Successful cyclists build a mileage base, strengthen their glutes, and select the most appropriate clothing. They experiment with foods and fluids for hydration and energy. They know which emergency gear to carry in their backpacks. And they have tools ready for unexpected roadside breakdowns.

They've been thoughtful and they're ready to ride the race.

If we're not willing to think through the ways we talk with students about standardized tests, we might as well pull out the test-preparation packets and go through them page by page by page. Keep teaching to the test. No time to think. No time to contemplate. Just riding on the rickety rim.

We've heard others say, "No one grows taller by being measured" or "Weighing the cows won't make 'em fatter." Both adages are true. There are other factors that determine our height and weight. Our sizes and shapes are as unique as our individual thumbprints. And ultimately, we can't forget that testing isn't all it's cracked up to be.

We take our first standardized test when we're only a few minutes old. Remember your child's Apgar scores? Did Virginia Apgar realize in 1952 that hospitals throughout the modern world would be rating a baby's appearance, pulse, responsiveness, muscle activity, and breathing using her scale? Probably not. But in every nursery, few new mothers are saying, "I can't believe Matilda scored only an eight. She should have tried harder on the Babinski. I hope she can get into Harvard." They're just glad to count ten fingers, ten toes, and relish the miracle. And soon, new milestones replace Matilda's measly eight on the Apgar: she sleeps through the night, takes her first steps, and says her first words. Her first standardized score fades from memory. So it is with most standardized tests.

And we ask ourselves, What can we do in the meantime?

Step out of the box. Our local and state tests cannot, nor will they ever, truly meet the needs of our students. Instructionally, the information we receive three or four months down the road can't affect our teaching today. We rely on other assessments and evaluations to give us more relevant data—we're smart that way, eh?

As educators, we can't strictly rely on the value others place on high-stakes tests. Instead, we value the strategies outlined in this book. We value the individual milestones of students who cross the thresholds of our classrooms each day. We value thinking.

Although we don't particularly value the current testing frenzy, we do believe all students can be encouraged to think through tests. *To put thinking to the test.* And we invite all our teaching colleagues to do the same.

Someone once said, "What you test is what you get."

In her poignant piece "Passing the Tests That Matter," Carol Wilcox gives us a glimpse of what matters to her during these harried times.

Passing the Tests That Matter
By Dr. Carol Wilcox
(reprinted from The Denver Post, *January 25, 2002)*

Four school days until the state reading test, and I am a woman on a mission. I punch the start button on the copy machine, then dash around the corner to the third-grade classroom to fill out a few more forms for the assessment department. From there, I will race to pick up my copies, then hustle to a fifth-grade classroom to work on test-taking strategies one more time.

Even in the mania of my mad dash, I notice Maria as soon as I cross the threshold of the third-grade classroom. Yesterday, this dark-haired sprite twirled gracefully across the room to show me her new pink gloves, shot with metallic thread and trimmed with fake fur. Today, however, she is not twirling or sparkling. Dark circles ring her eyes, her lower lip trembles. I think of the copy machine, the hours until the CSAP, the eight minutes until I am due in the fifth grade and ask what is wrong.

"I don't live in my house anymore," she says sadly, softly. "When I came home yesterday, my bed wasn't in my room. My bed is in an apartment." She continues, "My dad was the one that used to play with us. I can't ride my bike at the new apartment. Me and Josie and my dad used to ride bikes every day."

I have been a teacher a long time and know well the litany I am supposed to recite to children walking through the valley of the shadow of divorce. "Sometimes grownups have trouble. Just because they do not love each other anymore does not mean that they don't love you." And yet this chorus seems as inadequate as it always does. Like sticking a Band-aid on a brain tumor.

Maria's eyes well, and I think there will be many tears, but there are not. Her voice is soft and drawn. "First we were a happy family. And now we live somewhere else. My mom is going to tape my dad's number by the phone. And I can call him when I miss him. My dad will have Valentine's Day by himself. I was the only one in my family who had Christmas, and now my dad won't have Valentine's Day. He will be all by himself."

I shuffle the papers in my hand. Think of the CSAP next week. The forms that need to be filled out. The scores that will be published in the paper. The governor's new report cards. And then I think of the tests that really matter. I take Maria's hand, and we go to my office. I get out the construction paper and crayons, and Maria silently colors a picture for her dad. I can see a dog, tail wagging, a little girl waving. Spencer, in my office for the day on an in-house suspension, watches with the kind of holy, wide-eyed silence that children somehow seem to reserve for those that are hurting. Finally Maria is done. I watch as she carefully tapes together a crooked makeshift envelope, then writes, "Por Papa" [Spanish for "For Papa"] on the outside. Task complete, she is ready to return to her class.

The forms for the assessment department sit in a messy pile, unfinished, on the corner of my desk. The boxes of CSAP materials are not opened or sorted or counted. The fifth graders did not get their one last practice session. Twenty years from now, those will not be the tests that really matter. No one will remember that I missed the deadline on yet another "urgent" form from the assessment department. No one will remember the percentage of proficient, partially proficient, or unsatisfactory children at my school or any other. No one will remember whether the governor assigned our school an A or an F. But maybe, just maybe, Maria will remember that someone cared enough to hold her hand, to cry with her, to help her make sense of life's hard tests. It's not that I do not think the state reading tests are important. I do. It's not that I think that emotional issues or self esteem can or should replace academic rigor. I do not. But I choose, in this age of standards and test craziness, to pass the tests that really matter.

So what matters?

The spontaneity of chrysalises turning into butterflies. Wilbur greeting Charlotte's children. Creating three-dimensional shapes with marshmallows and toothpicks. Finding the perfect word to describe the sky's color after a rainstorm.

These things matter.

Writing a book about testing has been an experience. We were concerned it might appear to our readers that we'd joined the ranks of test proponents, believing testing takes precedence over learning. Because we know the time we have with students is precious, we also worried that this work would become one more thing added to educators' already full plates. We hope neither fear comes true.

We are hopeful that those of you who are trying to change the testing situation in our country won't give up. We are hopeful that those of you who are under administrative pressure to increase scores won't abandon everything you know about your students and their learning. We are hopeful that those of you who have ignored high-stakes testing will become more test savvy. We are hopeful that you won't give in to pressure.

We're just saying—think. Then we can all be satisfied that we've passed the test.

References

Afflerbach, P. 2004. *National Reading Conference Policy Brief: High Stakes Testing and Reading Assessment*. Oak Creek, WI: National Reading Conference.

Allen, J. 2002. "Test-Smart Language Users: Understanding the Language of Testing." *Voices from the Middle* 10 (1): 56–57.

Allison, J. 2005. "Biggest Upside to CSAP: No Homework." *Douglas County News Press*, April 7.

Bielenberg, B., and L. W. Fillmore. 2004. "The English They Need for the Test." *Education Leadership* 62 (4): 45–49.

Block, C., L. B. Gambrell, and M. Pressley, eds. 2002. *Improving Comprehension Instruction: Rethinking Research, Theory, and Classroom Practice*. San Francisco: Jossey-Bass.

Bomer, K. 2005. "Missing the Children: When Politics and Programs Impede Our Teaching." *Language Arts* 82 (3): 168–176.

Buckner, A. 2002. "Teaching in a World Focused on Testing." *Language Arts* 79 (3): 212–215.

Calkins, L., K. Montgomery, and D. Santman. 1998. *A Teacher's Guide to Standardized Reading Tests: Knowledge Is Power*. Portsmouth, NH: Heinemann.

Child, L. 2005. *Clarice Bean Spells Trouble*. Cambridge, MA: Candlewick Press.

Cummins, J. 2000. *Language, Power, and Pedagogy: Bilingual Children in the Crossfire*. Clevedon, UK: Multilingual Matters.

Dooley, C. M. 2005. "One Teacher's Resistance to the Pressures of Test Mentality." *Language Arts* 82 (3): 17–185.

Encarta World English Dictionary (North American Edition). 2007. Microsoft Corporation. http://encarta.msn.com/encnet/features/dictionary/dictionaryhome.aspx.

Graves, D. 2002. *Testing Is Not Teaching.* Portsmouth, NH: Heinemann.

Greene, A. H., and G. D. Melton. 2007. *Test Talk: Integrating Test Preparation into Reading Workshop.* Portland, ME: Stenhouse.

Grimes, S. 2006. *Reading Is Our Business: How Libraries Can Foster Reading Comprehension.* Chicago: American Library Association.

Harvey, S. 1998. *Nonfiction Matters: Reading, Writing, and Research in Grades 3–8.* Portland, ME: Stenhouse.

Harvey, S., and A. Goudvis. 2000. *Strategies That Work: Teaching Comprehension to Enhance Understanding.* Portland, ME: Stenhouse.

Harwayne, S. 2001. *Writing Through Childhood: Rethinking Process and Product.* Portsmouth, NH: Heinemann.

Heuser, D. 2002. *Reworking the Workshop: Math and Science Reform in the Primary Grades.* Portsmouth, NH: Heinemann.

Hillocks, G. 2003. "Fighting Back: Assessing the Assessments." *English Journal* 92 (4): 63–70.

Hyde, A. 2006. *Comprehending Math: Adapting Reading Strategies to Teach Mathematics, K–6.* Portsmouth, NH: Heinemann.

Keene, E. O., and S. Zimmermann. 1997. *Mosaic of Thought: Teaching Comprehension in a Reader's Workshop.* Portsmouth, NH: Heinemann.

———. 2007. *Mosaic of Thought: The Power of Comprehension Strategy Instruction.* Portsmouth, NH: Heinemann.

Kohn, A. 2004. *Practical Strategies to Save Our Schools.* http://www.alfiekohn.org/standards/strategies.htm.

Langer, J., E. Close, J. Angelis, and P. Preller. 2000. *Guidelines for Teaching Middle and High School Students to Read and Write Well: Six Features of Effective Instruction.* Albany, NY: CELA.

Mantione, R. D., and S. Smead. 2002. *Weaving Through Words: Using the Arts to Teach Comprehension.* Newark, DE: International Reading Association.

Miller, D. 2002. *Reading with Meaning: Teaching Comprehension in the Primary Grades.* Portland, ME: Stenhouse.

Morgan, B. 2005. *Writing Through the 'Tween Years: Supporting Writers, Grades 3–6.* Portland, ME: Stenhouse.

Newmann, F., A. S. Bryke, and J. Nagaoka. 2001. *Authentic Intellectual Work and Standardized Tests: Conflict of Co-Existence?* Chicago: Consortium on Chicago School Research.

Pearson, E. D., J. R. Roehler, J. A. Dole, and G. G. Duffy. 1992. "Developing Expertise in Reading Comprehension." In *What Research Has to Say About Reading Instruction,* eds. J. Samuels and A. Farstrup. Newark, DE: International Reading Association.

Plitt, B. 2004. "Teacher Dilemmas in a Time of Standards and Testing." *Phi Delta Kappan* 85 (10): 745–748.

Popham, W. J. 2004. "'Teaching to the Test' An Expression to Eliminate." *Education Leadership* 62 (3): 82–83.

Public Education & Business Coalition. 2004. *Thinking Strategies for Learners.* Denver, CO: Public Education & Business Coalition.

Quindlen, A. 2005. "Testing: One, Two, Three." *Newsweek,* June 13, 88.

Raphael, T. 1986. "Teaching Question and Answer Relationships." *Reading Teacher* 39: 516–522.

Ray, K. W. 1999. *Wondrous Words: Writers and Writing in the Elementary Classroom.* Urbana, IL: NCTE.

Ritchhart, R. 2002. *Intellectual Character: What It Is, Why It Matters, How to Get It.* San Francisco: Jossey-Bass.

Santman, D. 2002. "Teaching to the Test?: Test Preparation in the Reading Workshop." *Language Arts* 79 (3): 203–211.

Tovani, C. 2000. *I Read It, but I Don't Get It: Comprehension Strategies for Adolescent Readers.* Portland, ME: Stenhouse.

———. 2004. *Do I Really Have to Teach Reading?* Portland, ME: Stenhouse.

Trabasso, T., and E. Bouchard. 2002. "Teaching Readers How to Comprehend Text Strategically." In *Comprehension Instruction: Research-Based Best Practices,* ed. C. C. Block and M. Pressley. New York: Guilford.

Welty, E. 1979. *The Eye of the Story: Selected Essays and Reviews.* New York: Vintage Books.

Wilcox, C. 2002. "Passing the Tests That Matter." *The Denver Post,* January 25.

Wolf, S. A., and K. P. Wolf. 2002. "Teaching True and To the Test in Writing." *Language Arts* 79 (3): 229–240.

Zemelman, S., H. Daniels, and A. Hyde. 2005. *Best Practice: Today's Standards for Teaching & Learning in America's Schools.* Portsmouth, NH: Heinemann.

Zimmermann, S., and C. Hutchins. 2003. *7 Keys to Comprehension: How to Help Your Kids Read It and Get It!* New York: Three Rivers.